CENTURION
MAIN BATTLE TANK
1946 to present

A NOTE ABOUT THE TERM 'MAIN BATTLE TANK'

From its inception Centurion was designated as A41 Heavy Cruiser, but with the advent of Fighting Vehicle (FV) numbers it became Tank, Medium Gun, Centurion Mark 3 and so on up to Mark 13. The term 'Main Battle Tank' (MBT) only came into regular parlance with the introduction of Centurion's successor – FV4201 Chieftain MBT. Strictly speaking it is incorrect to call Centurion a Main Battle Tank but such has been its longevity that Centurion remains extant long after Chieftain or any of its variants have been withdrawn from service. It seems fitting, therefore, that the accolade of Main Battle Tank be applied to Centurion since it transmuted from Heavy Cruiser via Capital and Universal to Medium Gun Tank, so the term Main Battle Tank remains apposite as it embraces all these concepts of armoured warfare and is testament to a remarkable tank design.

Dedication – to Yzzy

First published in May 2017
Reprinted 2021 (twice) and August 2023

A catalogue record for this book is available from the British Library.

ISBN 978 1 78521 057 0

Library of Congress control no. 2016959356

Published by Haynes Group Limited,
Sparkford, Yeovil, Somerset BA22 7JJ, UK.
Tel: 01963 440635
Int. tel: +44 1963 440635
Website: www.haynes.com

Haynes North America Inc.,
2801 Townsgate Road, Suite 340,
Thousand Oaks, CA 91361.

Printed in Malaysia.

Commissioning Editor: Jonathan Falconer
Copy editor: Michelle Tilling
Proof reader: Penny Housden
Indexer: Peter Nicholson
Page design: James Robertson

COVER IMAGE:
Centurion Mark 3 Main Battle Tank.

CENTURION
MAIN BATTLE TANK
1946 to present

THE TANK MUSEUM

Owners' Workshop Manual

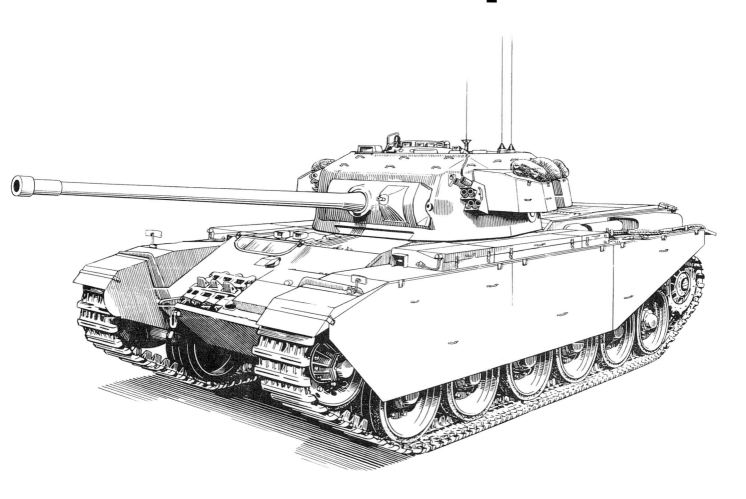

An insight into the design, construction, operation and maintenance of the British Army's most successful post-war tank

Simon Dunstan

Contents

OPPOSITE The primary attribute of any tank design is firepower in order to engage and destroy enemy armour on the battlefield. The 20-pounder main armament on Centurion proved to be a highly accurate and powerful weapon.

Author's preface

Tank – a simple, monosyllabic word that until a century ago was usually thought of as a water storage container. On 15 September 1916 that changed forever when the British Army employed a new weapon of war to break the stalemate on the Western Front that had been dominated by artillery and the machine gun. The tank was intended to change the face of warfare and that is what it did; but not in those early actions. The French also developed a similar weapon that they called *Char d'Assault Blindée* – Armoured Assault Vehicle: a far more emphatic term than 'tank'. For the Germans it was the *Sturmpanzerwagen* that meant much the same: five forceful syllables against just one for 'tank'. Yet tank is the name that has stood the test of time. From an unassuming

BELOW Thirty years of British tank development are encapsulated in a single frame as a Tank Mark V and a Centurion Mark 2 undertake a public demonstration at Bovington. Both machines were at the forefront of tank technology at the time of their introduction.

codename, the tank became the decisive land weapon system for the next century.

Within the British Army, the tank suffered a difficult and convoluted development following the First World War that continued into the Second World War. Only in the final days of the war did the Army receive a tank that had been sorely lacking in the heyday of the *Panzerwaffe* that epitomised Blitzkrieg and beyond. At last, the British fielded a tank that possessed an optimum combination of firepower, armour protection and mobility within the constraints of technology at the time. In the new-found tradition of naming tanks beginning with the letter C, it was called Centurion. Unlike its forebears, it was capable of being improved and upgraded repeatedly. This has been one of the main reasons for its longevity. Accepted into service with the British Army in December 1946, Centurion is still employed as a gun tank 70 years on by the South African National Defence Force under the name of Olifant.

Such durability is testament to an outstanding and flexible design that has evolved over the years into an exceptional battle tank with a host of diverse variants, many of which remain in service to this day. Despite its extraordinary history, there have been few books of note to recognise that fact. The present author has studied the subject of Centurion for many years and this volume represents the distillation of the research he has undertaken for the various books he has produced in the past which are no longer in print. Since this is ostensibly an Owners' Workshop Manual, it is only fitting that the individual users and crews give their views about life inside Centurion and all the vicissitudes that go with it. From fighting in the mountainous terrain of Korea in 1951 to the barren deserts of Iraq in 1991, Centurion was at the forefront in many wars across the globe. On every occasion, it was not found wanting. Furthermore, the crews of Centurion in every army forged an extraordinary bond with their own Centurion that was their home, their means of survival, their talisman and always their crucible of comradeship. It is hoped that this special combination of man and machine is reflected in these pages.

Author's note

U nless otherwise stated, all the photographs in this volume are from the archives of The Tank Museum, Bovington. Those annotated as IDF (Israel Defense Forces) are courtesy of the IDF Archives, the Israel Government Press Office and the IDF Spokesperson Unit, while those annotated SAAC (South African Armoured Corps) are courtesy of the Armour Formation South African National Defence Force.

The author wishes to express his gratitude to Brian Baxter of the REME Museum of Technology; John Brooker of the Puckapunyal Army Tank Museum; David Fletcher of The Tank Museum; Ian Maine of the Royal Marines Museum and Lieutenant Colonel Michael Mass of the Latrun Armored Corps Association Tank Museum as well as Matt Sampson, the photographer at Bovington Tank Museum.

Particular thanks are also due to Ken Brown 17/21L, Trevor Dady RTR, George Forty RTR, Keith Glenn RTR, Robert Millgate REME and Richard Swan RE for their invaluable contributions on the life and times of the Centurion in British Army service.

ABOVE **After 70 years of frontline service Centurion remains a potent MBT in the guise of the Olifant Mark 2, seen here displaying its highly effective camouflage scheme during a training exercise at de Brug Military Training Area near Bloemfontein, the home of the South African Armoured Corps. The tank incorporates extensive composite armour arrays and a highly sophisticated fire control system with all-weather thermal, day and night sights for the gunner and commander.** *(Photograph SAAC)*

Foreword

By Lieutenant Colonel George Forty OBE

Like most of my contemporaries in the Royal Armoured Corps I spent my formative years as a troop leader commanding a troop of four Centurions. I have the fondest memories of the Cent. I was therefore very touched by the sad ending of a 'Cent named OOBA', which Simon Dunstan chose to conclude this excellent and authoritative book. My affection for my own tank often manifested itself in words of comfort and praise, or of patting its armour plate affectionately, as a knight might have caressed his noble charger – has not every tankman done likewise at some time or another? I will always have the utmost respect and deep affection for the Centurion and so it is with the greatest pleasure that I write this foreword to introduce this outstanding book.

I first came into proper contact with the Centurion when I was commissioned, with three others, in August 1948 into the 1st Royal Tank Regiment, from the newly reopened Royal Military Academy Sandhurst. We had learned a great deal at Sandhurst and could command a brigade, division or corps with consummate ease, but sadly had very little idea on how to look after a troop of tanks and not a single clue about the inner mysteries of the Centurion. Nor did we have the excellent Young Officers' Special to Arms Course, which is now run at the Royal Armoured Corps Centre, Bovington, to give us a chance of gaining this knowledge, so we arrived at our regiment not knowing anything very much about practical tanking. Fortunately, the powers that be had appreciated this situation, and we were given our very own potted Young Officers' course, which included all aspects of driving, maintenance, gunnery, radio and of commanding and manoeuvring

RIGHT Lieutenant George Forty looks on quizzically from his commander's cupola as a print journalist is assisted into the driver's compartment during a press presentation on the re-formation of 6th Armoured Division in May 1951. As the officer commanding 1 Troop of B Squadron, 2nd Royal Tank Regiment (2 RTR), George Forty received the first Centurion tanks within the division.

a Centurion tank. 1RTR was stationed at Detmold in West Germany and we did much of our training in and around the Sennelager Training Area. I think that the initial and most lasting impression I gained of the Centurion from our course was of complete confidence in its strength and reliability. It was quite easy to understand, drive and maintain, even for someone like myself who was born with two left thumbs and very little mechanical aptitude. We were dealing with the very early marks of Centurion in those days, but I think the tank's relative simplicity has remained over the years, while its performance and reliability have been greatly improved. After our course we became tank troop leaders – does any other job ever really compare with the thrill of having a troop of tanks under one's command for the very first time? I doubt it – and we gleefully charged all over West Germany on various mammoth exercises. One of these exercises was, I remember, followed by a highly 'bulled up' parade for 'Manny' Shinwell, who was then War Minister. We had rushed back to barracks after the exercise, steam-cleaned the tanks all night by the light of arc lamps, loaded them on to transporters and moved out to the area of the Windmill on Sennelager for the parade with bewildering speed. A complete armoured division on parade is a marvellous sight, but mechanical failures could have spoilt the whole effect. Everything went off immaculately, however, thanks to the inherent reliability of the Centurion as much as anything else.

I left 1RTR late in 1949 for a brief spell as a radio instructor at the RAC Centre in Bovington and then found myself with 2RTR in Crookham, Hampshire, helping to train the 56th London TA Division who were equipped with Comet tanks. But not for long; 2RTR was soon released from its TA assistance role when 6th Armoured Division was being reformed and we moved to Tidworth to prepare for an eventual return to Germany. Because of my previous Centurion experience I had the great honour of having the very first troop of Centurions in the entire division. It is difficult to put down on paper just how my troop felt when we took over our four brand spanking new Cents. We quickly became the centre of attention within the regiment, indeed the number of envious

visitors was legion and we became quite blasé. I was even allowed to choose new names for my four beauties and did so calling them 'Black Prince' (mine), 'Black Adder' (not Baldrick), 'Black Arrow' and 'Black Knight'. Fanciful names perhaps, but nevertheless we thought that they were very appropriate! Never had any troop lavished so much care and attention on four tanks – so we fondly imagined. They were outstanding, did everything we asked them to do and were our pride and joy. Of course our moment of stardom was all too brief, as other troops in our squadron soon began to get their own new tanks. I remember seeing one hard-bitten staff sergeant closer to tears than it would have been thought possible when he received the news that the tank transporter carrying his particular Cent had overturned near Larkhill. He rushed out to see it and fortunately the damage was only superficial, but the sight of his brand new tank, now with twisted bins, bent mudguards and scratched paint, was just too much for him and he had to be physically prevented from assaulting the unfortunate tank transporter driver! We had some marvellous months of training. Working up with the division, for instance, we motored as a complete squadron, on our tracks, down from Tidworth to Lulworth in Dorset, for our annual firing on the Gunnery School ranges. Motoring through such towns as Shaftesbury was fantastic, the entire civilian population appeared to have turned out to watch our progress and to shower us with fruit and flowers – talk about conquering heroes! The boys loved it and the Cents, as usual, did their stuff with the minimum number of breakdowns en route. The range firing too was a great success, despite the fact that we did most of it wearing respirators. This was followed by the major divisional 'Agility' exercises, which took place all over the south of England, and were some of the most ambitious ever held in the UK since the war.

Once we reached BAOR [the British Army of the Rhine] I was made regimental Intelligence Officer, so swapped my beloved Cents for a Dingo scout car, and it was not until 1953 that I got back to troop leading again. This time I was with 1RTR in Korea, where it was war in earnest instead of exercises. I found it quite easy to

ABOVE In February 1952, 2 RTR moved from Tidworth to Munster in Germany as part of the deployment of 6th Armoured Division to BAOR. A series of major field exercises followed to bring the division up to full fighting strength to counter the perceived threat of the Soviet Union during the Cold War. Here, 1 Troop, B Squadron of 2 RTR takes part in such an exercise.

get back into the swing of things; the Cent had changed little, so it was quite like coming home. I took over a troop of tanks in C Squadron and when the regiment moved out of reserve and back into the line, we forded the Imjin River and took up positions in support of the Black Watch on the notorious Hook feature. I stayed there when they were relieved by the Duke of Wellington's Regiment, which for me was a great delight, as both my father and brother had served in the 'Dukes' in the First and Second World Wars respectively. I have many vivid memories of that period in the line, but I won't bore you with them here. From the Centurion's point of view, they were highlighted by two factors – firstly the extreme accuracy and lethality of the 20-pounder gun and secondly, the very real feeling of security once one was inside the tank and 'buttoned up', no matter what shot and shell was falling outside. We did a lot of night firing, using American searchlights to help us – they were fine until shot out, but really caned the vehicle batteries. We blessed the relative simplicity of the gun control equipment, because for much of the time, due to our round-the-clock activity, we could only afford to have two men manning the tank while the other two slept.

After an enforced absence in hospital, recovering from an argument with a Chinese mortar bomb – having foolishly deserted the safety of my Cent I hasten to add – it was back to Comets again for me as adjutant of a TA regiment, based in London. This was followed by a most enjoyable stint commanding 2RTR Reconnaissance Troop, so it was quite a few years before I was back to tanking again. This time I was second in command of Badger Squadron in 2RTR with responsibilities, among other things, for ensuring that the AFVs were regularly inspected and that the vehicle documents were properly kept up to date. I was very relieved to find that, despite some new features, the Centurion was still basically the same tank in which I had fought in Korea, so again it was like coming home. The reliability and ease of maintenance were once more very apparent. I should explain that throughout the period I have been talking about, my tank crews always consisted of a mixture of regulars and National Servicemen, and I don't think that any of them ever had the slightest difficulty in understanding the Centurion. Of course the more expert they became and the longer they stayed on the same tank, then the more they got to know its individual quirks and how to get the very best out of their own particular vehicle.

I did not get to command 'Badger' because I went off to brigade on a staff learners course, followed by Staff College and my first staff appointment. On my return to regimental duty I commanded an armoured car squadron, so it was not until my second staff tour, this time as an instructor at the RAC Tactical School, that I once again got back to tanks. The school was responsible for running tactical training for the Young Officers' courses, which I have mentioned. We took them out for a short period of practical tanking on Salisbury Plain to round off their course. In addition, we shared Lulworth Camp with the Gunnery School, so I was able to witness at first hand the devastating lethality of the L7 105mm gun, which was now installed on the Centurion. It is still one of the best tank guns in the world, as has been constantly proved by its performance in the various Middle East wars and elsewhere. By the next time I got back to regimental duty, the Centurion had been replaced by the Chieftain, so when

my regiment, 4th Royal Tank Regiment, converted from the armoured reconnaissance role to tanks, it was the Chieftain and not the Centurion we had to take over. I remember that my first reaction on looking inside a Chieftain turret was thinking how complicated the gun control equipment appeared after Centurion. Of course we all quickly became accustomed to the new gear, but it reinforced my opinion that one the main features of the Cent was its relative simplicity.

The last time I climbed on board an operational Centurion was in 1973, when I was lucky enough to be a member of a small party visiting the Israeli Armoured Corps for a few days. Despite the new powerpack and other mods, the signs in Hebrew and the sand-coloured camouflage paint, the Cent was still much the same as the one I had started my training on in Germany, 25 years before. Undoubtedly Centurion had been the main battle tank success story of the post-war era with its worldwide clientele of contented customers, and proving its superiority on the battlefield time and time again, not only over contemporary designs but over even more modern and supposedly more powerful opponents. Why has this been so? I believe it is because in the original design the ideal balance between the characteristics of firepower, protection and mobility were achieved. Some tank designs sacrifice armour for speed, while others have too much armour or too small a main armament, or are underpowered or have a poor transmission system. Centurion has been just about right from the very start, so although it has been constantly and sensibly improved, it has retained many of the original basic features. It has been a tank in which the crews of many nations have had supreme confidence and one with which many tankmen, like myself, have forged a deep bond of affection. For my part I shall never forget the thrill of sitting in the commander's seat while thundering across country, or watching with deep satisfaction as a hard target erupted in a vivid orange flash indicating a direct hit, or listening to enemy artillery shells bursting harmlessly outside and knowing that one was perfectly safe inside its armoured walls. Firepower, protection and mobility, that is what a tank is all about and the Centurion had the lot!

**IN MEMORIAM
GEORGE FORTY OBE 1927–2016**
CURATOR OF THE TANK MUSEUM 1981–94

ABOVE 02BA37 ARROMANCHES was Lieutenant George Forty's Centurion Mark 3 while serving with 1 RTR in 1953 during the Korean War, seen here on a 'lay-back' position on the Sausage feature with the glowering heights of The Hook to the left of picture. Above the 20-pounder gun is an American searchlight and the tank has a .50-calibre machine gun forward of the loader's hatches.

Chapter One

The Centurion story

The Centurion emerged as the synthesis of British tank design after six years of warfare. Originally conceived as a Cruiser Tank, it emerged as the Capital or Universal Tank that had been sorely lacking during the war. Its greatest strength lay in its ability to be upgraded time and again.

OPPOSITE With the distinctive black beret of the Royal Tank Regiment, crewmen relax beside a Centurion tank. The crew of any tank soon came to know each other's foibles in life but close teamwork was essential to the efficient working of Centurion. To many, Centurion was the quintessential 'tankman's tank' because of its simplicity of operation with its basic crash gearbox, mechanical connecting rods and levers that rarely went wrong.

The need for a new tank

In the late 1930s, priority in rearmament was given to the Royal Navy and the Royal Air Force for the defence of the British Isles against the threat posed by Nazi Germany. New equipments for the Army languished, particularly in tank design and development. Up until 1937/8, British Armoured Fighting Vehicles (AFVs) were primarily comprised of light tanks and armoured cars for police and garrison duties across Britain's far-flung Empire. Any new tank designs were fundamentally compromised by the arbitrary decision to limit their maximum weight to 18 tons to conform to railway loading regulations. At the outbreak of the Second World War in September 1939, British armoured forces around the world were composed of 834 Light Tanks Mark VI, 77 Cruiser Tanks Mark I A9 and 111 A13 and 66 Infantry Tanks Mark I.

After the fall of France in July 1940 and the British Army's withdrawal from Dunkirk, the only serviceable tanks available for the defence of Britain were 200 Light Tanks and 50 Infantry Tanks equipping 8th Battalion Royal Tank Regiment. With the loss of all its heavy equipment in France, the Field Army had to be reorganised, re-equipped and expanded from virtually nothing. With the real threat of invasion, the immediate requirement was to provide units with any and all types of weapons available, while those awaiting tanks were organised as mobile machine gun regiments mounted in trucks and light armoured cars or else manned improvised armoured trains.

The need for tanks in large numbers capable of operating in the defence of the country was now paramount. Every tank produced was taken off the assembly line for immediate issue to units awaiting equipment. No interference with production that would allow the introduction of major modifications or new designs was countenanced. Furthermore there was no time to undertake the engineering tests necessary to establish and improve the reliability of the main mechanical components of any existing or new design put into production.

Accordingly, the production of types in which there were known defects was continued regardless. Fresh manufacturing capacity was sought to produce new tank designs and this fell to engineering companies often with no previous experience of tank construction. The result was predictable, as foreseen at the time, with the emergence of several indifferent tank models that were chronically unreliable mechanically, particularly in the high heat and harsh conditions of the Western Desert. In the early battles, the existing tanks were so unreliable that the majority of casualties were due to mechanical failure.

During Operation Battleaxe to relieve Tobruk in June 1941, 7th Armoured Division – equipped with A9s, A10s and A13s – lost half its tanks on the first day of the approach march. By the end of the second day, the complement was reduced to two but only a few tanks had been destroyed in battle. It was decided to continue the attack with the remaining pair but as they moved off they collided with each other and for a time there were no serviceable tanks at all. It would have been risible if it had not been so tragic.

It was unusual for any regiment to arrive in battle with more than three-quarters of its tanks and very often the effective strength was much less. The recovery and repair of all these defective vehicles required great ingenuity and resourcefulness if the momentum of an attack was to be maintained. The problem was exacerbated by some appalling design features in the tanks. For instance, on almost every Crusader the external oil gallery on the crankcase leaked. This simple defect could be rectified in about 3 minutes, but it took two days to remove and reinstall the engine in field conditions so that the repair could be undertaken.

The General Staff was also aware of the urgent need for greater reliability, heavier armour and more powerful tank armament. By now the General Staff's overall requirement was for the armoured forces to be expanded to 12 Armoured Divisions and nine Army Tank Brigades. To this end, the Tank Board was formed in June 1940 to foster the design and development of British AFVs and related equipments. At the same time the post of Director General Armoured Fighting Vehicles (DGAFV) was created at the War Office, with the first incumbent being Major General Vyvyan Pope. His deputy (DDGAFV) was Mr Claude

Gibb, an Australian engineer and formerly director general of weapons and instruments production at the Ministry of Supply. In his own words he wished 'to move from making guns to making tanks'.

As DGAFV, Major General Pope established the Department of Tank Design (DTD) to co-ordinate the complete design and development cycle of any new tank, as well as modifications to existing vehicles. Nevertheless the design parentage of any AFV remained vested with the commercial company tasked with the implementation of the specification as determined by the General Staff. Together with the Experimental Wing DTD, these branches came under the auspices of the Ministry of Supply. Previously, tank design and supply were the responsibility of the Mechanisation Board under the Master General of the Ordnance. In addition there was the Wheeled Vehicles Experimental Establishment to develop armoured cars and all manner of support vehicles. In early 1942 the Experimental Wing DTD became the Fighting Vehicles Proving Establishment (FVPE) based at Farnborough.

At the outset, the priority of the DTD was to introduce a tank armed with a 6-pounder gun, given the limitations of the 2-pounder gun in face of the emerging German tank designs that featured such refinements as face-hardened armour and a highly capable 50mm main armament that easily outranged and outperformed the British 2-pounder, let alone the superiority of German optical sighting devices.

With delays plaguing the introduction of the A27M Cromwell Cruiser Tank Mark VIII armed with a 6-pounder gun, the first tank so armed was the A15 Crusader Mark III Cruiser Tank that appeared in May 1942 as a stop-gap measure. In the same month the A22 Churchill Mark III Infantry Tank IV was issued armed with the 6-pounder gun. Unhappily the Churchill was still too mechanically unreliable, the bane of British tanks to this point, for widespread service in the Middle East.

Providentially, armoured units in Egypt were now being issued with new American tanks such as the M3 Lee/Grant and M4 Sherman Medium Tanks armed with a dual-purpose 75mm gun in time for the decisive Battle of El Alamein in October 1942. The M4 Sherman was to remain the benchmark of Anglo-American tanks for the remainder of the war. It was produced in vast numbers at the rate of one every 4 minutes at the height of production in the newly created tank arsenals established across the United States.

ABOVE The A15 Crusader of 6 RTR, seen here in the North African desert, typified early war British tanks. As a Cruiser it was fast and lightly armoured. With a 2-pounder gun it possessed strong firepower for the 1940-41 period, but it suffered from poor reliability, especially in the desert, despite the best efforts of its users. *(Tank Museum)*

ABOVE The A27M Cromwell was the British late-war Cruiser tank. Its speed of 32mph, high mobility and low silhouette made it the tank of choice for armoured reconnaissance regiments in north-west Europe, but its thin armour was vulnerable to the most powerful German guns, and it did not have the firepower to outrange the latest German tanks.

One of the fundamental flaws of British tank procurement in the early years of the Second World War was the expectation that commercial engineering companies building buses or railway carriages could readily switch to the manufacture of complex AFVs. Vauxhall Motors were tasked with the design and manufacture of the A22 Churchill Infantry Tank IV. A difficult gestation and birth ensued before a mature tank eventually emerged fulfilling many roles on the battlefield. Similarly, the Birmingham Railway Carriage and Wagon Company became the design parent for the A27M Cromwell, together with Rolls-Royce Motors Limited.

As the design parent, a company was responsible for the complete development of a tank based on a General Staff Requirement with the DTD providing approval at all stages of manufacture or any modification to the original specification. The detailed inspection of components and sub-systems during construction to eliminate defects was also the responsibility of the manufacturer. However, the impetus for the output of tanks in quantity made manufacturers resistant to any interference with the production of the particular tank for which they were responsible.

The problems inherent in such a system were fully understood by the War Office but there was no real alternative since the Royal Navy had priority for heavy engineering resources and the Royal Air Force for high-performance engines; thus British tanks were fitted with First World War vintage Liberty engines or low-powered commercial ones such as the Meadows. As a result, delays into service of inadequately tested designs were all too familiar, including the Covenanter, Cavalier and Centaur. In October 1941, the War Office learned that the Cromwell, which was scheduled to begin series production in April 1942, would be delayed until the late summer or early autumn of 1942.

In fact production did not begin until February 1943 – too late to see action in the North African campaign. Nevertheless, by the time of the invasion of Normandy in June 1944, both the Cromwell Cruiser Tank and the Churchill Infantry Tank were the mainstays of the British armoured forces, together with large numbers of M4 Shermans. Many of the latter were armed with the potent 17-pounder gun in the guise of the Sherman Firefly. The latter was the only British or Anglo-American tank capable of engaging the Tiger 1 or Panther on anything like equal terms of firepower.

It is chastening to observe that virtually all British tanks produced during 1943 were either obsolete or obsolescent with the emergence of the Tiger 1 and the Panther or even the Panzer IV with its longer 75mm gun in the previous year.

COVENANTER	0.5%	Obsolete
CAVALIER	5%	Obsolete: half to be converted to OP tanks and half used for training
CENTAUR	17%	Obsolete: one-twelfth for use as Close Support tanks with the remainder used for training or conversion to tankdozer
CRUSADER	26%	Obsolete: two-thirds to be converted to Anti-Aircraft tanks and the remainder used for training
CROMWELL	7.5%	Obsolescent with 6-pounder gun. The first Cromwell to be armed with the 75mm gun was not fit for service until March 1944
MATILDA	2%	Obsolete
VALENTINE	24%	Obsolete: gun tanks mainly for the Soviet Union with some to be converted to SP guns, bridgelayers and DD amphibious tanks
CHURCHILL	18%	Obsolescent with 6-pounder gun although the tank proved successful during the Tunisian campaign. The first production version of Churchill with the 75mm gun was the Mark VI, besides the locally improvised Churchill NA75

Throughout this period there was little mechanism for front-line armoured soldiers, 'the Users', to have any input to the design process and thus what the User in the field actually required. Some serving officers were seconded to the DTD but their numbers were few and their influence limited due mainly to the need to expedite production quotas. In order to broaden the technical expertise among the Royal Armoured Corps, the School of Tank Technology (STT) was formed on 27 May 1942. As its name implies its purpose was to study and teach the technology of AFVs and the best methods for their employment in battle. The STT was based at a country house, Woodlee,

on the London Road at Egham, Surrey, a property appropriated by the Mechanisation Board in 1940.

The staff comprised a chief instructor with the rank of colonel, six officer instructors and 135 other ranks. Many of these came from the Fighting Vehicles Wing of the Military College of Science at Shrivenham. These personnel also provided technical expertise to the Director Royal Armoured Corps (DRAC) Users Committee and the DRAC Advisory Committee. Their remit included the study of captured enemy equipment and they were among the first to examine Tiger 1 '131', which resided in the Enemy AFV Section and was

LEFT The A22 Churchill was the Infantry tank used in north-west Europe. Armed with the same 75mm gun as the Cromwell, it was much slower at just 12½mph. Its cross-country mobility and armour protection proved excellent, however, making it valuable for infantry support.

inspected by hundreds of visitors. Interestingly, several of these equipments were subsequently given to the RAC Tank Museum at Bovington Camp in Dorset where the STT was based from 1951 onwards.

In late 1942, the STT moved to a purpose-designed establishment at Chobham Lane in Chertsey, Surrey, where it was co-located together with the DTD and FVPE. For the first time, the British Army had a coherent design centre for the development of AFVs and associated equipments. It was soon to prove its worth after several years of frustration and too many lacklustre tank models. With the consolidation of the design and testing departments at Chobham, the rank of commandant of the DTD and FVPE was upgraded from lieutenant colonel to brigadier, although the post was also open to suitably qualified civilians. Indeed, the appointment as Chief Engineer of the DTD was filled by Mr Albert 'Bill' Durrant, while the post of commandant at FVPE went to Brigadier Walter Morrogh. Both men were to be crucial to the design and development of the A41 Centurion.

In July 1940, a senior Royal Armoured Corps (RAC) officer was attached to the British Purchasing Commission in Washington DC to represent British AFV requirements to the United States and Canadian authorities. This eventually became the AFV Branch of the British Army Staff in America and was central to the procurement of M4 Shermans in large quantities under the Lend-Lease Program. It also led to the production of Sexton SPGs and Kangaroo APCs based on Canadian-designed vehicles that were used extensively by the British Army during the campaign in north-west Europe in 1944–45.

The first incumbent was Major General Douglas Pratt who had commanded 1st Army Tank Brigade (4th and 7th Royal Tank Regiments) during the Battle for France in 1940. As part of the Barnes Mission that co-ordinated all war production in the USA both for the American armed forces and for Lend-Lease to the Allies, General Pratt was party to the Anglo-American report of the 'AFV and Self-Propelled Artillery Group'. This document was considered and accepted at the 19th Meeting of the Tank Board on 16 September 1942. In its opening paragraph on tank policy, it stated:

The British and American staffs are in agreement that the major requirement is for an 'All-Purpose Tank', the standard components of which should provide the degree of flexibility required to mount the various types of tank armament in use or under development.

It is the present author's contention that this was the genesis of the A41 Centurion.

Designing the A41

In the same month, Commander Robert Micklem was appointed Chairman of the AFV Division of the Ministry of Supply and, at the same time, Chairman of the Tank Board. On secondment from Vickers-Armstrongs Limited, Commander Micklem was now directly responsible to the General Staff for the development and production of tanks and AFVs as well as research, design and testing. Thus, by late 1942, all the elements were finally in place for the co-ordinated design and development of tanks and other AFVs for the British Army.

The design of the Centurion was initiated under the designation A41 Heavy Cruiser, following the General Staff Long-Term Policy on the role of tanks formulated in the Army Council Secretariat Paper dated 8 September 1943. The General Staff maintained its belief that to fulfil the tactical role of the armoured forces, two categories of tanks were required: an Infantry Tank to breach the enemy's main defensive positions in conjunction with infantry and a Cruiser Tank to exploit the breakthrough and strike deep into the enemy's rear installations, either through gaps created by the assault of the Infantry Tanks or around the flanks. In addition, a class of specialised assault vehicles based on the Infantry and Cruiser Tanks was envisaged as bridgelayers, pillbox destroyers, amphibious tanks (and so on) following the failure of the Dieppe Raid in August 1942 when most of the attacking tanks were left stranded on the beach.

Under the short-term policy of the General Staff statement, the characteristics – in order of priority – of Cruiser Tanks intended to equip armoured reconnaissance regiments and

LEFT During the course of development of the A41 Heavy Cruiser, there was much discussion concerning the tank's secondary armament including the feasibility of a machine gun in the turret rear to provide automatic fire to the front when the main armament was secured in the travelling lock. This never materialised and a rear escape hatch cum main armament barrel replacement aperture was substituted.

armoured brigades of the standard armoured division were as follows:

1. RELIABILITY: The unhappy experience of British tanks in the Western Desert made the aspect of mechanical reliability of utmost importance to ensure the maximum efficiency of the tank under all conditions of terrain, temperature and sustained action.
2. DURABILITY: An initial life-mileage of at least 3,000 miles was deemed essential, coupled with simplicity of operation and ease of maintenance.
3. DIMENSIONS:
   Weight – to be under 40 tons.
   Overall width – not to exceed 10ft 8in and the optimum to be 10ft 4in, to enable the tank to negotiate Bailey bridges and to be readily transportable by rail.
4. ARMAMENT: The main armament to be of the high-velocity 75mm type, or such better gun as may be designed, to be mounted in a three-man turret. It was to be a dual-purpose weapon with highly effective High-Explosive (HE) performance, while at the same time being as effective as possible against enemy armour of the type likely to be encountered. Minimum acceptable performance to be the ability to penetrate 3.5in (90mm) at 30 degrees with APCBC (Armour-Piercing Capped Ballistic Cap) ammunition.
   A small proportion of tanks of the Cruiser class were to mount a weapon having superior Armour-Piercing performance in order to engage enemy AFVs with heavier armour than those against which the dual-purpose weapon was effective, being at the same time as effective as possible against anti-tank guns and other soft targets. A further proportion of tanks in every regiment were to mount a CS (Close Support) howitzer of the 95mm type or better, capable of firing HE, smoke and hollow-charge projectiles. In addition, a hull machine gun and a turret machine gun were required.
5. ARMOUR: Armour was to be the maximum possible, taking heed of the characteristics already laid down. A high standard of protection against the danger of fire was also essential.
6. SPEED AND ENDURANCE: Although the Cruiser Tank was to be capable of competing on even terms with enemy armoured formations, a high average speed and cross-country performance, including the ability to negotiate obstacles, was preferable to high maximum speed on roads. Endurance or radius of action was to be sufficient to enable an armoured brigade to operate at the greatest possible range and carry out its tactical role within a standard structure for replenishment of fuel and ammunition.
7. FIGHTING COMPARTMENT: The fighting efficiency of both main and subsidiary armament was of the utmost importance in the fighting compartment. The stowage and ease of handling of ammunition were factors of great importance especially in view of the increasing size of the ammunition to

ABOVE This overhead view shows the considerable overhang of the 17-pounder gun to the front that was a function of the required armour-piercing performance to defeat heavy German armour. Unlike previous Cruiser Tanks the commander and gunner of Centurion were situated on the right of the main armament; the gunner had his own hatches forward of the commander's cupola.

be handled. The turret and turret ring were to be of sufficient dimensions to enable the armament to be served with the minimum of fatigue to the crew.

Whereas the short-term policy necessarily implied modification and development of the existing AFV design – the A34 Comet – the long-term policy was to be, in principle, free from any such pragmatic restriction. The main General Staff Requirement was still for two types of tank to fulfil Cruiser and Infantry roles, but radically new principles of design were open to consideration with a view to obtaining better performance, penetration and protection.

At the 35th Meeting of the Tank Board held on 7 October 1943, the paper of 8 September was considered by the DRAC, the War Office and the representatives of the AFV Division of the Ministry of Supply. Despite a Defence Committee ruling that research and development for the war against Germany should be limited to projects for equipment which would be in the hands of the troops by the end of 1944, in order to concentrate on perfecting existing designs, it was recommended that long-term tank development should result in a machine to the following broad specification and its development be pursued with all urgency:

■ The weight limitation of 40 tons to be increased to 45 tons;
■ The turret ring to be not less than the 69in of the Sherman;
■ Meteor engine;
■ Merritt-Brown gearbox;
■ Armour: 4in frontal, side-maximum within

weight limitations. It was recommended that the side armour be not less than 60% of the frontal armour and, if possible, more. It was primarily for this reason that the weight limitation was raised to 45 tons;
■ In view of the considerable design improvements in protection afforded by a sloping glacis plate, together with increased space available for ammunition stowage, it was recommended that the design should not embody a hull machine gun;
■ The tank was to mount a 3in 17-pounder, with a coaxial machine gun, firing fixed ammunition and, if possible, provision was to be made for mounting as an alternative, a 32-pounder with separate ammunition and coaxial machine gun;
■ Wading ability of up to 6ft.

As a result of the criticism in Parliament and elsewhere of the manner in which tank design and production had been conducted, it was decided that the DTD was to prepare the new A41 (capable of satisfying the General Staff Long-Term Policy for the development of a Cruiser Tank to fulfil the roles previously stated).

Until this time, the DTD at Chobham had held two functions: in the first instance to act in the role of a consultant engineering organisation to all firms engaged in tank design and production with special emphasis on fighting equipment and immunity, and, secondly, to act as the inspector of current production models and to approve modifications rectifying defects in existing service vehicles. Over the years, the DTD had acquired such a fund of technical knowledge and experience that it was engaged at times on original design work for the manufacturers.

In the latter half of 1943, Mr Claude Gibb, an engineer and director of the Newcastle firm of Parsons, was on loan to the Ministry of Supply and became Deputy Director General of Armoured Fighting Vehicles. He was sufficiently impressed with the potentialities of the DTD that he entrusted it with the exclusive task of designing the tank, identified as A41, incorporating the fruits of its accumulated experience. However, in accordance with stated Government policy as approved by a Select Committee of the House of Commons, design responsibility, subject to approval by the DTD, was to remain with selected parent design firms, working in consultation with, and assisted by, the DTD where its experience enabled it to make a special contribution on matters of armament, protection and special problems associated with tracked vehicles. In the case of A41, design parentage was never clearly defined until mid-1945 when it was entrusted to Vickers-Armstrongs Limited of Newcastle, hence the A41 was primarily a product of the DTD.

As the responsibilities of the design parent included the production of technical drawings, parts lists and User handbooks, outside firms were approached to undertake this task, the DTD having no facilities for such work. The Associated Equipment Company Limited (AEC) of Southall, Middlesex, happened to have spare capacity in their drawing office at the time and agreed to produce plans under contract to the DTD. As the A41 programme progressed, AEC became involved with the design work on the suspension and subsequently assisted the DTD in the fabrication of the original 'soft-boat' A41 mock-up. Other firms were engaged as component design parents. These included David-Brown Limited of Huddersfield, responsible for the Merritt-Brown gearbox, and Rover Limited for the Meteor engine.

Already utilised in the Cromwell and Comet, the Meteor was a de-rated version of the Rolls-Royce Merlin engine that powered the Spitfire, Hurricane and a host of other famous aeroplanes. The conversion of Merlin to Meteor began in April 1941 with a prototype engine running in a Crusader at Aldershot during September. The 27-ton tank achieved

a top speed of 50mph over a half-mile course at a fuel consumption of 1.35mpg, with its elongated exhaust stacks glowing red-hot. The conversion was undertaken by a team of Rolls-Royce engineers at Clan Foundry at Belper under the direction of Mr Roy 'Rumpty' Robotham, ably assisted by Mr Fred Hardy who designed the cooling fan group. As the war progressed, Rolls-Royce Motors increasingly concentrated their efforts on the production of aircraft engines, so in January 1944 they passed production and development rights of the Meteor to Rover Limited in exchange for the latter's research into Frank Whittle's gas turbine jet engines. Nevertheless, the success of the Meteor as a tank engine prompted the DTD to persuade Roy Robotham to join the department as chief designer, where his experience was vital to the creation of Centurion.

Although it was too early to define specific details, the tactical requirements envisaged, coupled with the known factors concerning armament, available engine and gearbox, were such that the basic characteristics could be formulated. After many exploratory meetings, the basis of a provisional vehicle emerged. A small team of specialists in each field then took responsibility for direct detail investigation and design through a co-ordinating design team under the chairmanship of Claude Gibb. This team was responsible for the final vehicle layout. The respective groups dealt with hull and armour, turret, armament, engine and transmission and suspension.

The necessity of thwarting attacks by known anti-tank guns, including the dreaded 88mm, determined frontal and side armour thicknesses.

ABOVE The combination of the cast front and roll plate turret rear is shown to advantage here as well as the characteristic turret lifting eyes of the A41 and Centurion Mark 1. The offset uni-axial Besa machine gun could be fired independently by the loader/operator, or linked to the main armament for co-axial fire. Such a system increased the workload for the loader/operator to an unacceptable degree.

Apart from components such as engine, transmission and fuel tanks, where overall dimensions were known quantities and the space necessary for the main components and crew, this governed the basic hull size. Other factors governing hull dimensions were primarily the turret ring size and the position of the driver. The previous weight and dimension limitations, conformable to British railway loading gauge that had so constrained earlier British tank designs, had been waived by the War Office at the insistence of the DTD. The hull sides were sloped inwards to save weight and to minimise the effect of mines detonated by the tracks.

The basic dimensions of the turret were determined both by the degree of immunity to attack required and the turret ring diameter, dependent on the calibre of the main armament and gun recoil, as well as loading and firing requirements. To simplify production, a turret with a cast front and elsewhere of welded plate construction was chosen, although the desirability of an entirely cast turret was not overlooked.

The adoption of the 17-pounder anti-tank gun entailed no serious problems and an orthodox mounting was used, comprising gun cradle and protective block incorporating trunnions in the turret aperture with a mantlet providing protection at all angles of elevation. Here also, immunity to frontal attack determined the basic mantlet and block thicknesses. Within limitations, this arrangement offered the best chance of keeping the mounting operational after a direct hit to the frontal armour. There were diverse opinions as to the choice of auxiliary weapons; some favoured a quick-firing heavy-calibre gun, while others advocated an orthodox machine gun mounted either in the front and/or rear turret; or possibly a front mounting incorporating twin 7.92mm Besas.

With all these alternatives the problems associated with ammunition-feed, firing mechanisms and crew responsibilities increased in direct proportion with the calibre and number of guns. Pending a General Staff ruling on the subject, design work proceeded on the most difficult combination of a 20mm Polsten in a ball mounting alongside the main armament, with a Besa machine gun mounted in the rear of the turret.

The General Staff Requirement for the Meteor engine offered an adequate combination of power, flexibility and development potentiality. The Meteor Mark 4 was compact enough that both it and the proposed transmission system could be located together in the rear hull with direct output to the final drives and sprockets at the vehicle rear whilst still allowing the main armament sufficient depression over the engine deck.

It was decided to redesign the Z5 Merritt-Brown gearbox, used on the Cromwell and Comet, in order to improve its performance for A41. A differential lock to assist in extricating the tank when one track slipped, a dry sump with jet lubrication of all gears and a reversed rotation output shaft combined with a new double reduction final drive gear system were specially designed for the vehicle under the designation Z51. In addition, the opportunity was taken to improve loading and gear-changing characteristics. Five forward and two reverse gears delivered power through a differential gear train to provide brake steering control. This basic system had proved to have the lowest transmission losses and gave maximum possible power at the sprocket.

Several suspension systems were considered, but a type designed by Mr George 'John' Rackham, Chief Engineer of the Associated Equipment Company of Southall, adapted from a basic design by S.A. Horstmann that was developed by Vickers-Armstrongs, was adopted. This system was chosen in relation to the hull shape to obtain maximum flexibility, reliability, ease of maintenance and cross-country performance, while giving the required ride characteristics. Due allowance was also made for the increased vehicle weight likely to occur with future development in armour and armament.

The Christie suspension of earlier Cruiser Tanks was discounted because the increased weight exceeded its effectiveness. A torsion bar system was not chosen because it was deemed too vulnerable to mine damage and, as it required internal volume, would have raised the height of the hull (and, as a consequence, the vehicle weight to an unacceptable degree). The modified Horstmann system embodied large roadwheels ensuring long tyre life and by mounting these in twin axle arms operating against a single set of double-acting horizontal coil springs in three bogies on each hull side, a compact and accessible arrangement was achieved. The system also served to give greater protection to the hull as it was externally mounted.

One notable innovation was the provision of an auxiliary 3kW generator, driven by an 8hp Morris engine, to ensure a reserve of electrical power for radios, battery charging and gun control equipment. The fighting compartment was also pressure ventilated to remove fumes, eliminate flashback and protect the crew against gas. To ensure reliability, no hydraulic or pneumatic systems were employed and simple mechanical rod controls were used throughout for the change-speed mechanism, clutch, differential lock and brakes.

As design work progressed, a provisional specification was submitted for the consideration of the Tank Board at their 36th Meeting on 22 November 1943. It was the view of the AFV Division that the development and subsequent manufacture of A41 could, at a certain stage, be conveniently handed over to Leyland Motors to follow on as the next step after the A34 Comet. Considerable discussion took place as to when A41 could be introduced into production. After Leyland Motors had stated their views, the meeting was adjourned until 23 November in order to enable the Ministry of Supply and the General Staff to give the matter further consideration.

On the resumption of the meeting, the Ministry of Supply recommended that arrangements would be made for the design and production of prototypes to be carried out entirely independently of Leyland Motors; that the aim would be to produce pilot and pre-production models towards the end of 1944 and, provided no undue difficulties arose, small-scale production would start in the second quarter of 1945. The Deputy Chief of the Imperial General Staff (DCIGS), Lieutenant General Sir R. Weeks, then requested further information on the A41. The specification was tabled and discussed. Full particulars were then set out in R.T.B. 123 (43) and after further discussion, DCIGS advised the Chairman, Commander Robert Micklem, that he would

endeavour to obtain a War Office decision as soon as possible. On 26 November the DCIGS informed the Board that the War Office were in agreement with the recommendations and development was to proceed accordingly.

At their 37th Meeting on 30 December 1943, the Tank Board discussed a further provisional specification of A41 R.T.B. 125 (43). As the DRAC was unable to give a final decision on the armament and other features, the first mock-up was being prepared for the most complex combination of armament – the 17-pounder main gun with 20mm Polsten on separate trunnions and one Besa in the rear of the turret. In a minute to the Chairman of the Board dated 22 January 1944, the DRAC agreed with A41 proceeding on the basis of a 17-pounder and Polsten 20mm. On 11 February he stated that he had now taken the opportunity of discussing the A41 specification in more detail with a number of Users and that there was an insistent demand for a machine gun capable of sustained firing to the front.

Although the advantages of a 20mm were realised, especially for penetrating the gunshields of anti-tank guns, a 20mm was not considered an adequate alternative to a Besa, nor was it felt that the Besa mounted in the rear of the turret in any way compensated for the lack of one mounted in the front. Moreover, the 30-round 20mm magazine used in AA (Anti-Aircraft) tanks had been rejected as being unable to give a sufficiently sustained rate of fire. A machine gun was required capable of engaging personnel and the 780 rounds of 20mm ammunition contemplated were totally insufficient for such a task. He therefore asked if it was possible to mount a Besa coaxially with the 17-pounder in conjunction with a Polsten in the left-hand side of the turret.

A four-man turret was proposed in order to provide sufficient crew to employ such a diversity of weapons, but this was not pursued. A suggestion to reduce the radius of action to 72 miles was deemed most unacceptable because the Users were accustomed to a range of 125 miles in the Cromwell and Sherman and said it would entail additional transport in the echelon.

There was in addition a firm User demand for a high-speed reverse gearbox. This request came from experience of operating tanks in the orange groves and sunken roads of southern

Italy. Vehicles had often been ambushed in such areas and being unable to manoeuvre freely many were lost when they exposed their vulnerable flanks while attempting to turn round. A high-speed reverse was required to enable the tanks to withdraw rapidly. This was a remarkable instance of a particular and peculiar set of circumstances leading to an addition to the original design at the behest of the User. The modified gearbox was designed Z51R (R for high-speed reverse) and was incorporated into production vehicles.

The A41 was the first British tank to be designed in consultation with the User during the early stages of development to ensure that the first prototype vehicles should be as near to the final requirement as possible, thus eliminating major modifications at a later date. In the dark days of 1941 and 1942 it had been impossible to second experienced tank officers to the firms involved in the design and manufacture of tanks, and as a result of this many defects that might have been avoided at the design stage were built into production vehicles.

A final specification for the A41 R.T.B.131 (44) was considered and accepted at the 38th Meeting of the Tank Board held on 23 February 1944. The Board recommended that the Ministry of Supply initiate the production of 20 prototypes to the following configurations:

15 to mount   1 × 17-pounder
              1 × 20mm
              1 × 7.92mm Besa (in turret rear)
with Merritt-Brown Z51 gearboxes.
5 to mount   1 × 17-pounder
             2 × 7.92mm to front
             1 × 7.92mm to rear
with Sinclair self-shifting, self-synchronising pre-selective Traction Clutch Gearbox with Scoop Tube Coupling.

This gearbox was to incorporate six speeds forward and three reverse, with a maximum speed backwards of 14mph. This ingenious but extremely ambitious project was, however, still at an early stage of design and was regarded as highly experimental.

The Board further stated that A41 had their full support and should proceed with all possible expedition. Accordingly, the Ministry of Supply ordered 20 prototypes and two hulls to be manufactured besides the original 'soft-boat' mock-up. As there were no facilities for further work at AEC of Southall, production was assigned to the Royal Ordnance Factories (ROF) of Woolwich Arsenal and Nottingham, with sub-assemblies from ROFs Patricroft, Radcliffe and Ellesmere Port. Ten of the prototypes and the two hulls were to be built at Woolwich Arsenal and ten at Nottingham. The two supplementary hulls included an unarmoured mobile test bed – a 'soft-boat', which was of mild steel and with no turret, to prove the suspension, mechanical controls, engine and transmission layout and to guide final design. The other was a completely stowed armour hull and turret for 'firing at' trials for immunity acceptance.

At the 39th Meeting of the Tank Board on 4 May 1944 the question of the main armament for A41 was discussed and the priority was stated as follows:

1. 17-pounder 2. 77mm 3. 95mm Howitzer

On 24 May 1944, an Extraordinary Meeting of the DRAC's Advisory Committee was held at AEC Limited to discuss the A41. After the meeting had viewed the mock-up, a short discussion was held and the consensus of opinion was that the secondary armament must either be coaxial with the main armament or be capable of being linked coaxially with it. The number of support mantlets for each weapon in the turret was considered sound, especially as the loader could operate the secondary armament independently of the gunner. As a result, the order for the 20 pilot models was amended to be armed as follows:

1–5.   1 × 17-pounder, 1 × 20mm Polsten, 1 × 7.92mm Besa in ball mounting in rear of turret (first specification interpretation)
6–10.   1 × 17-pounder, 1 × 20mm Polsten with optional linkage and with rear escape door
11–15. 1 × 17-pounder, single Besa with optional linkage and rear escape door
16–20. 1 × 77mm, single Besa with optional linkage and rear escape door

LEFT AND BELOW
A41 P3 incorporated a 20mm Polsten cannon as secondary armament. The Polsten was of Polish origin but based on the Swiss 20mm Oerlikon design. Although an effective weapon against many battlefield targets that did not merit engagement from the 17-pounder main armament, the Polsten was an unwieldy device inside a tank turret and again distracted the loader/operator from his principal crew tasks.

During development it had been discovered that in order to accommodate the mounting of the Besa in the back of the turret it was necessary to omit the 2in bomb thrower and the rear escape hatch. It also entailed the relocation of the wireless set and re-stowage of Polsten magazines. As the rear Besa was not a General Staff Requirement but the 2in bomb thrower was, the DRAC ordered that production tanks would omit the Besa and incorporate the bomb thrower, but that it was unnecessary to alter prototype Nos 1–5.

On 8 June 1944, the committee was convened under the chairmanship of the Deputy Director of the Royal Armoured Corps and a User proposal was discussed to mount a forward machine gun to be operated by the driver, at the expense of ten rounds of ammunition, and the meeting agreed that five pilot models Nos 16–20 should be fitted with such a gun, either a Besa or a Bren with a 100-round magazine. Although firing trials were conducted in June 1945 of a prototype so equipped, the requirement was subsequently dropped. The meeting confirmed that the 20 pilot models were being produced as experimental tanks, but owing to difficulties in stowage and mounting it was not possible to incorporate the rear-firing machine gun. Thus, the scheme was abandoned.

At the 40th Meeting of the Tank Board on 15 June 1944 there was further discussion of the merit of the 77mm for A41 as it remained a firm User requirement for its superior HE round. The minutes, however, read:

Director General of Artillery [DG of A] questioned the advisability of fitting this gun in these vehicles since its performance was inferior to the 17-pounder which could be carried. It was explained that the General Staff had in mind the use of the 77mm gun in a proportion of these vehicles because of the greater ease in handling ammunition and the possibility of obtaining a higher rate of fire. In DG of A's view this difference would be small. The governing factor being the rate of laying. It was agreed that this point should be further considered before a final decision was taken on armament of these vehicles but no delay would ensue as all effort was being concentrated on the development of the vehicles mounting 17-pounder[s].

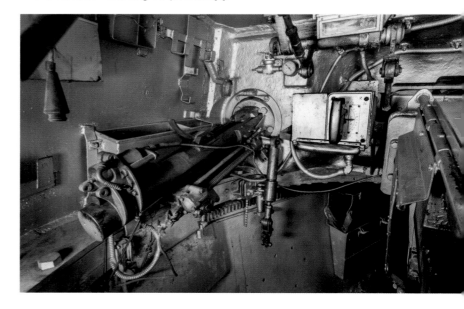

During September 1944, development trials of a 'soft-boat' hull, built at the DTD workshops in conjunction with AEC, began at the Fighting Vehicles Proving Establishment at Chobham. Although it suffered from 'tracking', which led to excessive wear of the steering brakes due to frequent corrections for road camber, there were no involuntary stops in the first trials. Further problems were experienced from pitching motions of the hull but as nothing was fundamentally wrong, production of the prototypes began in January 1945.

Meanwhile, design work had proceeded apace and new ideas were constantly being explored. In particular the advantages offered by a fully cast turret and the simplification of a coaxially mounted machine gun were pursued. To this end, the DTD, in conjunction with Vickers-Armstrongs, had been working on such a turret and it was incorporated on the A41A Cruiser Tank. On 19 January at the 21st Meeting of the DRAC's Advisory Committee at Chobham, the members viewed and discussed the mock-up of the A41A. This vehicle comprised an uparmoured A41 hull with a new turret embodying thicker armour and a new cupola with all-round vision devices, periscopic binoculars and a 22in commander's hatch. The cast turret enabled a superior designed shape with armour concentrated where it was most required, with minimum additional weight due to the neutral blending of contours. Furthermore, provision for machining and fitting of ancillaries became simpler with more freedom of location due to the absence of the weld seam between the cast front and the roll plate rear of the A41 turret.

Operation Sentry

In April 1945, the first A41 prototype was delivered to FVPE from ROF Woolwich Arsenal and performance trials began immediately. By this time the A41 had acquired the name Centurion, which had originally been allocated to the A30, a lengthened Cromwell chassis mounting a 17-pounder gun that was latterly named Challenger. At the first trial, Pilot No 1 covered 1,055 miles of which 467 were cross-country. Vehicle weight was 45 tons 11cwt and 2qtrs. A maximum speed of 23.7mph was recorded.

Prior to the completion of the trial, it was decided to prove a number of prototypes under active service conditions so that lessons could be learned and applied to production vehicles. Codenamed Operation Sentry, the object was

RIGHT A41 P3 T352412 was built at Royal Ordnance Factory (ROF) Woolwich Arsenal. The latter had been the main development centre of tanks for the British Army during the interwar years. Suffice it to say most of the designs were of an indifferent nature and it was not until the emergence of the A41 Centurion that the British Army received a truly battleworthy tank.

RIGHT At the rear of P3's turret is an escape hatch and the cable reel for 100ft of D10 communication wire. The A41 prototypes were fitted with 20in-wide tracks manufactured by Curran Steel Ltd. The black and white vertical stripes were illuminated at night as a convoy distance marker so that a following tank could keep at a safe interval when moving on road marches.

BELOW T352412 is shown in travelling configuration with its turret reversed to minimise its overall length. This would be used on uncontested roads or for transportation. At this stage there was no gun stabilisation system for Centurion so there is no gun crutch to secure the main armament.

RIGHT AND BELOW The driver's compartment of P8 T352415 shows the layout of the controls, which hardly differed on all Centurion models, with the gear control lever in the centre and the steering tillers to each side. The handbrake (far right) is below the instrument panel. Also visible from left to right are the clutch, brake and accelerator pedals, which like all the controls were actuated by simple mechanical rods and levers.

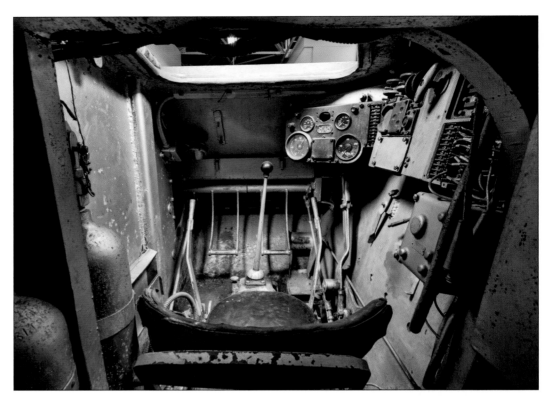

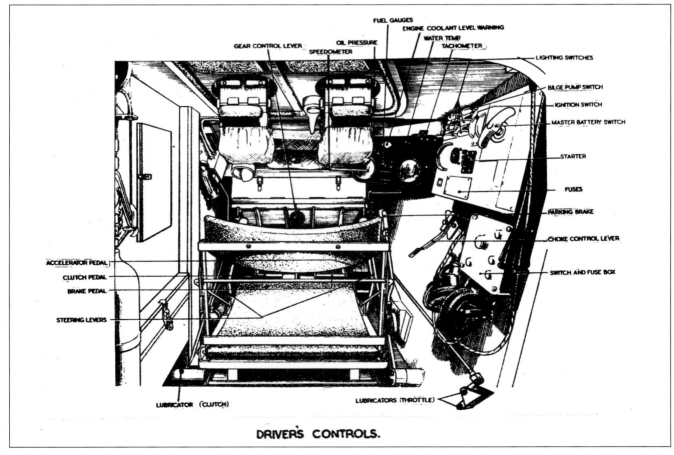

FUEL GAUGES
ENGINE COOLANT LEVEL WARNING
WATER TEMP
TACHOMETER
OIL PRESSURE
GEAR CONTROL LEVER
SPEEDOMETER
LIGHTING SWITCHES
BILGE PUMP SWITCH
IGNITION SWITCH
MASTER BATTERY SWITCH
STARTER
FUSES
PARKING BRAKE
CHOKE CONTROL LEVER
SWITCH AND FUSE BOX
ACCELERATOR PEDAL
CLUTCH PEDAL
BRAKE PEDAL
STEERING LEVERS
LUBRICATOR (CLUTCH)
LUBRICATORS (THROTTLE)

DRIVER'S CONTROLS.

to place Centurion prototypes in the hands of operational troops before the cessation of hostilities in north-west Europe. This was an unprecedented and imaginative idea, but VE Day came before it could be realised.

In the event, six new prototype Centurion tanks, three from ROF Woolwich Arsenal (P3 T352412, P9 T352416, P11 T352417) and three from ROF Nottingham (P4 T352413, P6 T352414, P8 T352415), were taken over at FVPE early in May by a detachment of the Guards Armoured Division, drawn from the Grenadier Guards, Coldstream Guards, Irish Guards and Welsh Guards, under the command of Captain Sir Martin Beckett MC, Welsh Guards. After training at FVPE and instruction at the AFV School Gunnery Wing, Lulworth, the party proceeded to Southampton on 13 May accompanied by a maintenance detachment from FVPE and 99th Ordnance Field Park which carried spare parts for the tanks. The following day, the Centurions embarked on two tank landing craft (LCT 789, Lieutenant C.D. Mitchell and LCT 1035, Sub-Lieutenant K.F. Bowe) and sailed for Antwerp, where they disembarked on 19 May.

Three days later a march of 443 miles up to the 7th Armoured Division began via Nijmegen,

ABOVE Early versions of Centurion had an extended hull with extra louvres for the cooling air outlet. Designated 'Long Hull', many were subsequently converted to become Armoured Recovery Vehicles. Centurion Marks 1 and 2 also featured strengthening ribs on the transmission covers as increased protection from artillery rounds or mortar bombs striking the rear decks.

BELOW In 1945 six A41 prototypes were rushed to Germany in an operation codenamed Sentry for testing under operational conditions, but the war ended before they could be deployed in combat. With the name SHEILA emblazoned on the side, T352417 was Prototype No 11 armed with a 20mm Polsten cannon as secondary armament.

ABOVE **One of the most distinctive visual aspects of Centurion were the skirting plates to protect the suspension from artillery fragments and hollow-charge weapons like the Panzerfaust, widely used in the latter stages of the war (hence they were commonly known as 'bazooka plates'). However, they were heavy and difficult to detach or re-attach if damaged or distorted in wooded terrain or accidents.**

across the Rhine to Osnabrück, Bremen, Hamburg and on to Gribbohm just short of the Kiel Canal. The party was attached for troop trials to the 22nd Armoured Brigade and divided its time between the 5th Royal Inniskilling Dragoon Guards (31 May to 11 June) and 5th Royal Tank Regiment (12 June to 23 June) under instruction from the Guards detachment. Tactical exercises were conducted by both regiments in comparison with Shermans and Cromwells.

Although both exercises were of a simple nature, they proved that, from a User's point of view, the tactical handling qualities were satisfactory. The Centurions were reasonably easy to conceal and, interestingly, those with side plates were less easily discerned than those without. Side plates, commonly referred to as 'bazooka plates', had been incorporated into the design after experiences in the closing stages of the war. Following the Rhine crossings, 34% of all British tank casualties had been at the hands of infantry weapons of the hollow-charge type, such as the Panzerfaust and Panzerschreck. The side plates gave some hull protection from these weapons. Gearbox whine, particularly in second gear, was noticeable and betrayed the position of the Centurion up to 1,000yd away, but the engine was remarkably quiet when kept off the governor limit.

The Users missed the acceleration of the Cromwell when executing tactical bounds and making for cover. Across country, the Centurion was found to give a comfortable ride and could negotiate obstacles extremely well, climbing inclines of 1 in 3 and descending slopes of 1 in 1 under full control. As regards

track-throwing, despite having 20in prototype tracks, the Centurion was successful in ground which would, and in one case did, throw a Cromwell track. Users questioned whether the Centurion had sufficient road speed for long marches, but it is interesting to note that on a forced march of 100 miles an average speed of 20mph was attained by a troop of three tanks with no mechanical trouble. Furthermore, on eight occasions the whole detachment covered 80 miles or more in the day, three of them being over 100 miles and the longest 120 miles. Based on experiences during the advance across north-west Europe, few occasions arose when mileages in excess of these were required.

Bogging trials were also held, attended by representatives of the Mud Committee, between two Centurions, a Cromwell, a Sherman and a Chaffee. The latter, with its speed, light ground pressure and automatic gear change did best, with Cromwell next, then Centurion and finally Sherman. In general, the performance of the Centurions with 20in tracks was very creditable and it was considered that with 24in production tracks and an improved gear change between 2nd and 1st gears, Centurion would be superior to Cromwell. The trial did, however, emphasise the need for a more powerful recovery vehicle than the Scammell or Cromwell ARV for recovery of the heavier Centurion.

On 8 June, cross-country races were held between two Centurions, two Cromwells and two Shermans over 1,000yd of undulating heather and heath interspersed with gulleys containing thick undergrowth and trees of up to 3in diameter. In the first race the two Cromwells won easily, followed by the Centurions and then the Shermans; for the next race handicaps were given of 0 seconds to the Shermans, 36 seconds to the Centurions and 1 minute 44 seconds to the Cromwells. The result was a dead heat between a Sherman and a Cromwell with a Centurion half a length behind and the remaining three tanks all within two lengths.

Between 27 June and 14 July, gunnery trials were held at the Lommel range in Belgium. User opinion of the fighting abilities of Centurion was high with only minor criticism of the ammunition stowage in the 30-round forward bin. A preference was stated for the Lucas power traverse over the Metadyne type. The turret pressurisation system was rejected as impractical since no crews wished to close down completely and an alternative method of expelling fumes from the fighting compartment was required. All Users requested a Browning instead of the Besa machine gun on account of the former's greater reliability. Also it was considered essential for the commander to have a Browning mounted on the cupola. Only one of the six Centurion prototypes was fitted with a Besa, the others having the 20mm Polsten, which was considered unsatisfactory as it intruded too far into the available turret space.

In general, mechanical defects were conspicuous by their absence and a distance of 2,300 miles, including 250 cross-country of comparatively trouble-free running, was achieved on the original tracks with only a few bogie tyre defects. Major component failures included three gearboxes, one main engine and a broken auxiliary engine quill shaft; a minor problem that was to plague Centurion for several years. Pilot No 11 suffered a sheared front idler bracket; a defect experienced by many early Centurions but which was easily rectified. Petrol consumption up to 1,442 miles, taken on an average of all six tanks, was 0.7mpg. After this period petrol was supplied in bulk and consumption could not be accurately measured.

Throughout Operation Sentry, every opportunity was taken to show the Centurion to representatives of other units of 21st Army Group including 2nd Army, 8 Corps, Guards Armoured Division, 79th Armoured Division, 4th Armoured and 34th Armoured Brigade. The operation was regarded as thoroughly representative as far as the Users were concerned and they considered Centurion the best tank they had ever had. They would have been prepared to go into action with them if they had been fitted with machine guns instead of Polstens. Performance, reliability, fighting characteristics and ease of maintenance were all considered satisfactory and the Users welcomed the opportunity, which they had not had before, to express their opinion on production prototypes, a procedure that has been maintained ever since.

On 21 July, the party motored to Ostend and on to Calais where four Centurions embarked by LCT for Dover and returned to FVPE on the 24th. The remainder of the party embarked on two LCTs on the 25th, disembarked at Dover and arrived at FVPE on the same day. The recommendations put forward by 22nd Armoured Brigade at the completion of Operation Sentry were considered at the 22nd Meeting of the DRAC's Advisory Committee held on 22 August 1945. As none of the criticisms were of major importance and in the main called only for enhanced handling and maintenance characteristics, a production programme of 800 Centurions was authorised. These were to include 100 Centurion Mark 1s (A41*) mounting a 17-pounder with a linked 7.92mm Besa and the remainder Centurion Mark 2s (A41A) of which the first 100 were to have 17-pounders and later versions 20-pounders.

With the defeat of Germany, the urgency of the Centurion programme diminished. During the months immediately following the war an assessment was made, based on the production capacity in hand, of the number of tanks required to re-equip the peacetime army. By November, the requirements of the Royal Armoured Corps were set at 2,077 for the proposed 1946 Order of Battle to replace Cromwells, Comets and Churchills by Centurions, excluding any consideration for Dominion or Allied needs. The plan provided for 480 Centurions during 1946 to be included in the 1946/47 Army Estimates. At a production rate of 40 per month, the Army would be re-equipped within five years.

To provide 50% reserves for the regular Army – and this was considered to be the bare minimum – as well as training vehicles for the reserves, would take between nine and ten years. For a programme of this magnitude it was necessary to obtain Cabinet approval, but at a meeting of the Defence Committee on 8 February 1946 the financial axe fell. It was agreed: 'that for the time being the output of tanks should be reduced to the minimum to maintain two tank factories in production'. This effectively cut production to 20 per month, at which rate it would take some fifteen years to fulfil the Army requirements for Centurions.

History seemed to be repeating itself. Treasury policy was unwittingly echoing the curtailment of the Medium D at the close

ABOVE The Centurion Mark 1 was fitted with 24in-wide tracks as against 20in on the A41 prototypes, giving the tank an overall width of 11ft to conform to the dimensions of Bailey bridges. Note that the smoke candle fitment on the rear cooling air deflector has been discarded now that the tank has smoke grenade dischargers on each side of the turret front.

BELOW T351700 was the first Centurion Mark 1 to be built at the ROF Woolwich Arsenal. This frontal aspect shows the now standard Centurion features of the spare track links on the glacis plate and the hooded headlights between them with the driver's folding windscreen at top left. Note the gunner's telescopic sight to the left of the 17-pounder gun mantlet and the Besa machine gun.

of the First World War. The repetition of the Treasury veto, due in both cases to the need to retrench after war, augured ill for the future for in fifteen years Centurion would be considered obsolescent and in all probability occupy much the same position as the Vickers Medium of the interwar years. The lessons of the 1920s and '30s, when the nation's defences had been allowed to wither, had obviously not been absorbed and the need to maintain a high standard of equipment to keep the Army at a reasonable degree of readiness was again being ignored. When compared with the expenditure demanded by total war the budget proposed by the War Office of £6,300,000 per annum did not appear to be excessive.

By 1946 12 A41 prototypes had been built. In the interim, extensive running trials and development of components had continued on test rigs and in vehicles. Up to this period, evolution of design had remained in step with these developments although it was rarely possible to embody the latest ideas in pilot vehicles currently being built. A total of 16 A41 prototypes were completed, including one A41S incorporating the SSS Powerflow gearbox. The remainder featured Merritt-Brown Z51 gearboxes and 17-pounder guns with various combinations of auxiliary armament, ten with 20mm Polstens and five with 7.92mm Besas.

Production

When production of Centurion began in November 1945 the basic design was stabilised. Prototype No 12 was reworked to Centurion Mark 1 standard and subjected to full-scale trials as stipulated in AFV Memorandum 4004. These trials covered specifically, performance and reliability, gearbox and engine cooling, defects and maintenance, turret power traverse characteristics and suspension. The trials were in three stages of 1,000 miles each and extended over a period of 18 months. The information gained was to influence future design and, in many cases, warrant modifications to those Centurions currently being built.

The production programme had been beset with delays, due primarily to a lack of electrical equipment. The first Centurion did not appear

ABOVE The Centurion Mark 2 was manufactured concurrently with the Mark 1, principally at ROF Barnbow, and 250 were built. The major change from the Mark 1 was the cast turret with a separate roof plate to provide greater ballistic protection; armour thickness of the gun mantlet was increased from 5in to 6in; and larger stowage bins were incorporated that were such a distinctive feature of Centurion.

RIGHT T351415 was one of the first Centurions Mark 2 to be deployed to Germany in 1947, touring armoured units of BAOR to familiarise them with the new battle tank. The Mark 2 was armed with the Ordnance, Quick Firing 17-pounder No 1 Mark 6 tank gun of 3in-bore diameter. Secondary armament was the 7.92mm Besa machine gun mounted coaxially beside the main armament with the gun mantlet encased in a canvas cover.

LEFT With its skirting plates removed, T351415 displays the Hortsmann suspension comprising six individual units each incorporating three helical springs arranged concentrically. The front and rear suspension units included shock absorbers with arms and connecting rods linking the shock absorbers to the suspension arms. Each suspension unit had two pairs of rubber-tyred roadwheels with six pairs on each side of the vehicle.

Centurion Mark 1 embodied a standard telescope linked to the gun mounting and gun control was by manual elevation and electric power traverse. The power traverse equipment was of the Lucas type and incorporated a variable speed control. This enabled the turret to be moved very slowly for fine laying or alternatively at a high speed when traversing a large angle. The turret was traversed by using one of three controls located close to the positions normally occupied by the loader, gunner and commander. The commander's controller overrode those of both the gunner and loader. The latter had the ability for power traverse to enable him to engage opportunity targets when the separate uniaxial machine gun mounting was not linked to the main armament. The gunner's periscopic sight of Centurion Mark 2, besides providing superior optical accuracy, incorporated integral range gear. As a result of it being mounted in the turret roof, installation was simplified and a vulnerable aperture in the frontal armour of the mantlet eliminated. The range gear with an integral range-drum enabled the gunner to read the range scale graduated for APDS (Armour-Piercing Discarding Sabot) and APCBC through the left eyepiece of the periscope. A sight clinometer was added to permit accurate indirect fire. A major innovation on later Centurions Mark 2 was the stabilisation of the main armament in azimuth and elevation. The first 50 Centurions Mark 2 were not equipped with this device. The Metrovick stabilisation system built by Metropolitan-Vickers Limited at Radcliffe Park enabled the gunner to hold the gun on or near the target, irrespective of hull movement. A raised strengthening web on the rear portion of the hull acted as a gun depression stop preventing the gun from fouling the hull when in the stabilised mode. Due to the shortage of rubber, the original models had either a metal or wooden gun depression rail. In the manual mode, it was not possible to traverse through 360 degrees if the main armament was depressed 4 degrees or more below the horizontal. Traverse was stopped over a range of 89 degrees to the rear of the vehicle by means of a cam-operated switch.

until February 1946. Both Centurion Mark 1 (A41*) and Centurion Mark 2 (A41A) were manufactured simultaneously, the production of the 100 Centurions Mark 1 being shared between ROFs Woolwich Arsenal and Nottingham. Three Centurions Mark 1 were built at ROF Barnbow, Leeds, which had recently been converted to tank production. Centurions Mark 2 were built at Vickers-Armstrongs Limited at Elswick Works, Newcastle, and ROF Barnbow at Leeds.

Marks 1 and 2

Centurion Mark 2 incorporated several major improvements, which could not be readily embodied in the Mark 1. These included a cast turret, commander's vision cupola, combined gunner's periscopic sight and range gear and a coaxially mounted machine gun. The latter, being integral with the main armament mounting and governed by the same control systems, relieved the auxiliary gunner of his role and enabled him to concentrate as loader-cum-wireless operator, besides eliminating the components of a separate mounting. The adoption of the commander's vision cupola (No 2 Mark 1) and the gunner's periscopic sight (No 1 Mark 1) did much to improve fighting efficiency. The two most vital factors of tank gunnery contributing to the defeat of enemy armour are accuracy of gun sighting equipment and speed of engagement. These are dependent on the ability of rapid target acquisition and an efficient fire control system.

Development of engine components had enhanced reliability and performance and, although of a minor nature in themselves, the many modifications combined to achieve considerable improvement overall. The piston compression ratio was raised from 6:1 to 7:1 to take full advantage of 80-octane petrol, thereby increasing engine output to 635bhp from the original 600bhp of the Meteor Mark 4. The new engine was designated Meteor Mark 4A. To offset the increased weight of 48 tons over the 46 tons 4cwt of Centurion Mark 1, the final drive reduction ratio was increased from 6.94:1 to 7.47:1. One of the factors which led to this change was the necessity not to overload the steering brakes and increase steering effort. As a result the maximum speed was reduced from 23.7mph to 21.42mph. The gear change between 2nd and 1st gears was modified to enable more rapid gear-changing in difficult terrain.

Close Support Centurion

In line with previous practice, the War Office had expressed a requirement for a Centurion mounting a high-trajectory howitzer to act in the close-support role during operations. The vehicle was to embody a 95mm howitzer firing HE and smoke ammunition at relatively short ranges. It was proposed to mount this weapon in 10% of Centurions. A wooden mock-up was prepared, based on an A41A but without provision for stabilisation of the main armament as it was not a General Staff Requirement. It was completed by December 1945.

Development proceeded slowly under the designation Centurion Mark 4. The problems of stowage for the number of rounds required and the design of numerous new components that differed from the standard gun tank caused considerable delays. It was not until March 1947 that a prototype Centurion Mark 4 was ready for inspection by DRAC's User Committee. It was in fact a Centurion Mark 1

ABOVE AND LEFT
One of the significant advances of Centurion was the Cupola, Vision, No 1 Mark 2 that gave the commander an all-round view of the outside terrain from under armour (a facility that German tanks had enjoyed throughout the war). The rotatable vision cupola incorporated eight episcopes with seven fixed No 5 Mark 1 and one No 6 Mark 1 elevating and extending episcope.

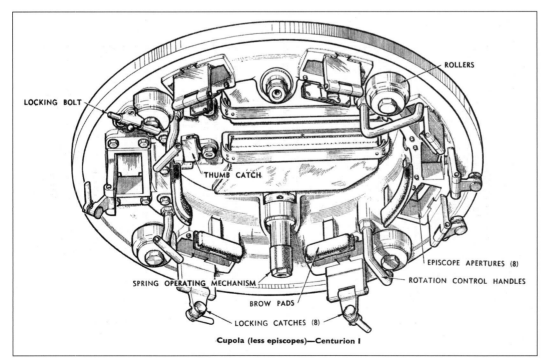

Cupola (less episcopes)—Centurion I

LOCKING BOLT

ROLLERS

THUMB CATCH

SPRING OPERATING MECHANISM

EPISCOPE APERTURES (8)

ROTATION CONTROL HANDLES

BROW PADS

LOCKING CATCHES (8)

modified to the close support role at FVRDE (Fighting Vehicles Research and Development Establishment, formerly FVPE). The 95mm and coaxial 7.92mm Besa were manually controlled in elevation with electric power traverse for the turret together with a special gunner's sight and range gear. The stowage of 'ready' rounds was criticised, but this was considered a minor deficiency. Firing trials were authorised to be undertaken in Kirkcudbright, Scotland. It was proposed to cease production of Centurion Mark 1 until such time as the 95mm howitzers and mountings became available. It was realised, however, that this decision was likely to lead to serious dislocation at the Royal Ordnance Factories as the production lines had been specifically laid down for Centurion Mark 1. Moreover, ROFs Woolwich Arsenal and Nottingham had experienced production difficulties, which caused delays in the supply of Centurion gun tanks into service with the Army.

In addition, as the number of 17-pounder guns already manufactured was in excess of requirements, no money was to be saved by cancelling Centurion Mark 1. In due course the cost of conversion to Centurion Mark 4 would have to be faced. It was decided to continue production of Centurion Mark 1 as a gun tank mounting 17-pounders as fast as possible, but at a later date 80 Centurions Mark 1 were to be withdrawn from service for conversion to Centurion Mark 4. Although in the event a rework programme was planned whereby ROF Barnbow was to convert Centurions Mark 1 and production of components began, in early 1949 the requirement of Centurion Mark 4 was cancelled by the War Office when it was realised that Centurion Mark 3 was able to fulfil the role by virtue of the performance of the new 20-pounder high-explosive ammunition.

Mark 3

By 1947, the 20-pounder anti-tank gun, first conceived as a 21-pounder in 1945, was in the final stages of design. Concurrently, design effort had been directed to embody the new gun in a vehicle designated Centurion Mark 3. These were identical with those that had already been approved for Centurion Mark 2. The method of ammunition stowage was based on careful design to minimise the risk of fire following wartime experience where the destruction of the majority of tanks had been due to ammunition fires. Research had demonstrated that a tank's chances of survival markedly increased when all the main armament rounds were stowed below the level of the turret ring. Such an arrangement was embodied in Centurion. The arrangement of 20-pounder ammunition stowage was similar to that of 17-pounder on Centurion Mark 2 with the exception of two extra armoured 'ready' bins which accommodated two rounds each. These were necessary because only two 'ready' rounds (as opposed to four on Centurion Mark 2 and five on Centurion Mark 1) could be accommodated in the turntable bin by reason of the larger-calibre gun.

As the Centurion Mark 3 hull was similar to Centurion Mark 2, only a wooden mock-up of the turret was prepared. It was viewed at FVRDE, Chobham, on 3 October 1946 at the 24th Meeting of DRACs Advisory Committee. On account of the larger ammunition, 65 rounds of 20-pounder were stowed as against 73 of the 17-pounder on Centurion Mark 2. During development up to this stage, the goal had been towards mechanical improvement at the cost of some increase in weight. Detailed calculations, followed by physical checks, established that this had increased disproportionately. The engine air outlet louvres were redesigned and the hull shortened by 4½in, thereby reducing weight by 100lb. By further scaling-down of dimensions, where safety factors permitted, and the elimination of the strengthening ribs on the transmission covers, the battle weight of Centurion Mark 3 was kept to 49 tons 5cwt. At the same time, other new design features, impracticable in the current production programme, were incorporated in Centurion Mark 3, although many modifications were constantly being made in production. More than 400 refinements were approved during this period.

Centurion Mark 3, while basically a Mark 2 as far as suspension, hull and turret were concerned, embodied several improvements. Besides the 20-pounder gun and revised stowage, the main features were the Meteor Mark 4B engine and more advanced gun control equipment. This complex equipment was progressively enhanced over a long period. A detailed summary would be onerous; suffice to say the main components such as gyro inductor units, tachometer unit, amplifier, alternator, metadyne and so on, had been brought to a high standard of efficiency. This type designated FVGCE (Fighting Vehicle Gun Control Equipment) No 1 Mark 3/1 was fitted in early production Centurions Mark 3. The Meteor Mark 4B had been improved in many ways over the Mark 4A and now developed 640bhp at 2,550rpm. Apart from a number of minor modifications, it now incorporated an additional dynamo to provide an alternative method of charging the batteries as well as more efficient fan belt tensioners and oil filter. Production of Centurion Mark 3 began in 1948 at Vickers-Armstrongs and ROF Barnbow.

Unsuccessful upgrades

Among the many schemes that were constantly being investigated during this period for Centurion, two are worthy of note. On account of the limited foundry capacity to produce the one-piece turret casting, an alternative turret was considered for Centurion and also to provide experience for possible future designs; 25 turrets cast in three separate parts were designed as planned. The first prototype passed ballistic tests but the difficulties of welding such large pieces and their subsequent heat treatment to meet immunity requirements proved this idea to be impracticable for large-scale production.

The second scheme was the SSS Powerflow transmission. The General Staff had expressed a requirement for the process of gear-changing of tanks to be made easier without at the same time resorting to designs that were complicated and costly in man hours to produce. The intention was to evaluate the Sinclair-Meadows SSS transmission as a possible alternative to the Merritt-Brown for later marks of Centurion and heavier classes of vehicles. The initials SSS stood for 'Synchro Self-Shifting'.

The Hydraulic Coupling and Engineering Company was given a contract for the supply of six gearboxes to be fitted in five Centurion prototypes. Unfortunately its layout and bulk

was such that it was not possible to install the gearbox in the same space as the Merritt-Brown Z51 and a modification was necessary to the rear portion of the hull, hence the different vehicle designation A41S. The only prototype completed with the SSS transmission was delivered from Woolwich Arsenal in September 1945 and was subjected to maker's development assessments until August 1947 when it was handed over to FVRDE for performance and reliability trials.

Many failures of the gearbox occurred, some of which caused appreciable damage. Gearbox No 1 was written off after 547 miles. Gearbox No 2 completed 1,092 miles but had many components replaced during this mileage. On account of the many breakdowns, no comparative trials with a standard Centurion were achieved. The SSS gearbox was appreciably heavier than the Merritt-Brown, weighting 3,520lb with the fluid coupling, as against 2,550lb of the Z51R and clutch. The greater bulk also necessitated a larger transmission compartment and thus some increase in hull weight.

Apart from the unreliability of the transmission it was not popular with drivers as it involved a different and unorthodox driving technique. It was never a serious contender for use in Centurion but was an interesting project that gives an insight into the problems of tank development, which often lead up blind alleys of research.

Proposed replacements

It is now pertinent to consider the saga of the A45. This vehicle was conceived as an infantry support tank to complement the A41 Heavy Cruiser with which it was to share a number of common assemblies. This followed a decision by the Tank Board in 1942 to implement a degree of standardisation between the two classes of vehicles. The A45 was intended to replace the Meteor-powered A43 Black Prince; an attempt to marry a 17-pounder gun in an enlarged turret on a widened Churchill hull. Development of A45 began in 1944 under the design parentage of the English Electric Company. The configuration was similar to A41 but overall dimensions were greater and armour thickness substantially increased.

ABOVE Intended as the replacement for the A43 Black Prince and as the infantry support tank to Centurion, the A45 was deemed part of the A41 programme. With heavier armour than the A41, this A45 prototype mounts a Centurion Mark 2 turret armed with a 17-pounder gun. The tank had a crew of five with the co-driver operating the remotely controlled Besa machine gun in the housing on the front track guard.

RIGHT At 55 tons the FV201 gun tank was considerably heavier than Centurion, yet it mounted the same main armament. As development of the FV200 series continued it was found that the basic hull could not readily be converted for all the proposed specialised roles, so only the gun tank was proceeded with as the FV221 Caernarvon.

The specification was altered following the recommendation in General Montgomery's Memorandum on British Armour: No 2, dated 21 February 1945, to abandon the unsatisfactory division of Cruiser and Infantry types and to develop a 'Capital Tank'. This was defined as a dual-purpose tank, suitable for operating within the armoured division and for support of the infantry. Throughout the campaign in north-west Europe the Churchill and Sherman had proved to be successful in both roles, as well as being adaptable into a multitude of specialised purposes such as flamethrowers, amphibious tanks and mine flails. In September 1946 this concept was formalised in a requirement for a Universal Tank capable of conversion to specialist tasks with the minimum of modification. The General Staff considered that Centurion could not be adapted to fulfil these ancillary roles without comprehensive redesign and the A45 was chosen as the basis for the series under the designation FV201.

Thus by December 1946, the month Centurion entered service with the British Army, the decision had been taken to supersede it by FV201. Until such time as the latter became available, production of Centurion was to continue. The first prototype ran in October 1947. Design of the many variants in the series proceeded at low priority. It was soon discovered, however, that the flail tank version needed a hull somewhat larger than the basic FV201, so a special vehicle would be developed. The universal concept was further compromised when it was found that both the gun tank fitted with DD equipment and the FV208 Bridgelayer were too tall to be launched from the LCT8 landing craft then in service. By 1949 such were the delays in the development programme, it was considered that when FV201 entered service it would be incapable of meeting the potential Soviet threat and it was cancelled in favour of Centurion, which was to be developed further. Combat effectiveness trials had shown that Centurion Mark 3 was superior to both the IS-3 and T-34/85 owing primarily to its superior fire control system.

RIGHT The definitive heavy gun tank emerged as the FV214 Conqueror armed with an L1 120mm rifled gun with a sophisticated fire control system featuring a coincidence rangefinder incorporated into the commander's rotating sub-turret. At 65 tons, Conqueror was powered by a modified Meteor M120 engine with fuel injection producing 810bhp with an operating range of 100 miles.

The preponderance of Soviet heavy tanks, however, led to a requirement for a 120mm gun to be mounted on the FV200 chassis to engage them at ranges beyond the capability of Centurion. Development was undertaken by the English Electric Company of such a vehicle designated Heavy Gun Tank FV214, Conqueror. Pending its introduction, a number of improvised tank destroyers were designed on the Centurion chassis, namely the Conway and FV4005. As the Conqueror hull and automotive components were essentially similar to FV201, only the 120mm turret had to be designed from scratch.

To gain experience of operating such large vehicles, five chassis were fitted with the Centurion Mark 3 turret on an adaptor ring under the designation Medium Gun Tank FV221, Caernarvon. The first prototype of this vehicle was running by April 1952. Production of Conqueror began in 1955 and it entered service in 1956. Thus the so-called universal tank to supersede Centurion finally emerged as a specialised long-range tank destroyer, with only one of the ambitious series of variants, FV219 ARV, to see service. As a final irony, the performance of the L7 105mm gun subsequently fitted to Centurion obviated the need for a heavy tank such as Conqueror with its restricted mobility and high servicing loads. It was withdrawn from service in 1966.

Into service

The Centurion was accepted for service with the British Army in December 1946. The first regiment to receive the tank was 5th Royal Tank Regiment of 22nd Armoured Brigade, 7th Armoured Division, based at Hamm in Germany. Initially only a limited number of Marks 1 and 2 were deployed during March 1947 in order to gain operational experience. A cadre of instructors was formed early in 1947, and by the end of that year the three regiments of 22nd Armoured Brigade (1 and 5RTR and 5th Royal Inniskilling Dragoon Guards) were all equipped with some Centurions.

In the early days, as with all new and complex military equipment, there was a host of teething problems – many of a minor nature, which after six years of wartime tank design should have been eliminated at the development stage. Automotive reliability was poor. There were many failures of the gearbox due to seizure of the gear oil pump, and gearbox casings cracked as a result of weaknesses in manufacture. Poor maintenance led to radiators clogging with accumulated dust and oil, causing overheating. Failures of coolant sealing rings of the Meteor engine, as a result of

BELOW A Centurion Mark 3 is put through its paces for a television programme with the presenter Raymond Baxter in the commander's cupola. A former wartime Spitfire pilot, Baxter was a keen proponent of British technology and is best known for the BBC television series *Tomorrow's World.*

ABOVE Despite its many attributes, one negative aspect of Centurion was the changing of major assemblies in the field. An engine change (shown here) took many hours and it was standard practice to backload tank casualties so that they could be undertaken in a proper workshop. In the field it could take at least 24 hours to change an engine even with a four-man REME team and suitable lifting gear.

BELOW The primary shortcomings of Centurion in the early years were its high fuel consumption and limited range of less than 50 miles on one load of fuel. REME workshops in Germany devised supplementary petrol tanks to be attached to the rear hull plate, but these were easily damaged when manoeuvring in wooded terrain or in road traffic accidents, causing fuel leakages and fires.

overheating, led to limited engine life. Magneto failures were widespread, while damp caused arcing that ruined points and led to persistent radio interference. The auxiliary charging engine overheated due to airlocks in the cooling circuit, and its splined quill shaft to the generator broke repeatedly. Oil leaked into the steering brakes, degrading performance. Track link circlips and washers broke, causing track pins to work loose inwards; there they were sheared by the hull, resulting in broken tracks. Axle-arm oil seals leaked. Lack of lubrication of the tensioning idler wheel caused it to seize and the idler-wheel mounting bracket bolts sheared under heavy load, with the result that the bracket and idler wheel fell off the hull. There were also many faults with gun mountings and sight gear. The turret hand traverse gear tended to bind when the vehicle stood at an angle; the turret was also liable to jam due to distortion of the inflatable sealing ring, and freeing it required removal of the turret. Communications were plagued by No 19 wireless sets of advanced age and dubious condition.

However, the most pressing problem was the limited operational road range of only 60 miles. This was highlighted during the Berlin blockade of 1948–49, when it was appreciated that Centurion would have been unable to reach the Inner German Border let alone the beleaguered city without refuelling en route. To overcome the problem a number of improvised spare fuel tanks were mounted on the rear hull in the manner adopted by Soviet tank designs. The original type was simply a 45-gallon fuel drum strapped to the rear plate, but this flimsy expedient easily ruptured in convoy collisions or when reversed into trees or buildings. Many variations on this theme were made at unit level before a jettisonable 180-gallon oval fuel tank, fabricated at the Hamburg Local Manufacture Unit, became standard equipment. An official design by FVRDE of twin jettisonable 40-gallon drums mounted on a cradle over the cooling air outlet was introduced, but proved unpopular with crews as it lacked the simplicity of local designs and curtailed depression of the main armament over the rear decks. Later an armoured mono-wheel fuel trailer was designed and widely used.

It was not until the introduction of Centurion

Mark 3 in 1948 that the Royal Armoured Corps received a tank with the superiority of firepower it had lacked throughout the war. When firing APDS Mark 3 ammunition, the performance of the 20-pounder gun (designed at the Armament Research and Development Establishment, Fort Halstead) was superior to any contemporary tank gun.

Wider User experience in the late 1940s resolved many of the earlier problems, and by 1950 Centurion was a reliable and effective fighting machine. There remained a number of minor irritations, such as the top-loading trackguard stowage bins that were difficult to reach from ground level and which often filled with water due to poor sealing of the lids. The commander's cupola hatch had a weak retaining pin in the vertical position, and many a commander suffered the loss of fingertips or concussion when it fell forward unexpectedly. These and similar faults were rectified both in the field and during production (side-loading stowage bins were introduced in late 1950), together with a multitude of other modifications to enhance performance. One worthy of note was an additional front track support roller introduced in 1948, to prevent damage to the outer shock absorber lever at No 1 suspension station.

Further development

By 1950 the production of Centurion Mark 3 was well under way, but operational use had demonstrated the need for further improvements. Up to this time nearly 100 design meetings had been held and approximately 250 major and minor modifications had been approved for the Mark 3 programme. Among the modifications instituted in late 1950 was the relocation of the loader's hatches to provide easier access and escape. The loader's periscope was moved forward on to the sloping face of the turret roof, while the 2in bomb thrower remained in its original position. At the same time the escape hatch in the rear of the turret was discontinued. The original purpose of this door had been to allow replacement of the 17-pounder barrel on Centurion Mark 2. This laborious process necessitated the removal of the commander's

cupola, lifting the breech block through the roof aperture, and finally pulling the barrel through the rear of the turret. With the advent of the 20-pounder, the barrel was so designed that it could be withdrawn forwards, which saved a considerable amount of time and eliminated the need for a rear door in the turret. Many earlier Centurions subsequently had the rear door welded shut, thus improving the armour integrity of the turret. One of the competitions among tank regiments in the 1950s was to see which could achieve the quickest 20-pounder barrel change. The fastest recorded time was 3 minutes 58 seconds by the 4th Hussars.

The Mono-trailer

The problem of Centurion's limited range was only partially resolved by the use of unarmoured external supplementary fuel tanks, and a more ambitious solution was devised by FVRDE in the form of a 200-gallon armoured fuel trailer towed behind the tank. Built by Joseph Sankey Ltd, this entered service in 1953, and there is no doubt that of all the equipment associated with Centurion none was more cordially loathed by tank crews.

The main problem was the excessive length of the vehicle with the Mono-trailer fitted. It created reversing problems, and it was difficult to negotiate through woods or in and out of firing positions. There were instances when trailers folded up on to the rear decks of tanks as they reversed up inclines. Conversely, it was possible to run over the trailer in reverse if it fell into a hollow. Petrol spillage was commonplace, through either pump malfunction or broken fuel hoses. This effectively immobilised the tank on public roads, since a spark from the metal tracks might ignite the petrol; many a traffic jam was caused on the roads around the Soltau training area by tanks halted by spillage and obliged to wait until the petrol had completely evaporated. Since there was no automatic cut-off switch on the trailer pump, it was possible for petrol to be pumped into the Centurion's fuel tanks when they were already full. This caused petrol to spill out of the fuel tank breather-holes and into the engine compartment, and several Centurions burnt out completely when this happened.

Coupling the trailer to the tank was a major task, since only one lifting ratchet was provided although two were desirable; this often led to distortion of the trailing arms. Peacetime restrictions did not allow for disengagement of the trailers by explosives, and they were towed throughout exercises even when empty; this caused them to buck wildly behind the tank, again distorting or breaking the trailing arms and making them nearly impossible to

uncouple. In one instance, however, this was perhaps fortunate. In the 1950s, before the general introduction of armoured personnel carriers, infantry were carried on tanks. The infantrymen were required to leap from tanks moving at speeds of up to 15mph. Accidents, unsurprisingly, were not infrequent. Unaccustomed to the intricacies of tanks, infantrymen might sit on the red-hot exhaust pipes, or their gaiter straps might become entangled with equipment latches as they jumped, suspending them from the tanks with their heads only inches from the tracks. On one occasion an infantryman decided to vault off the back of a Centurion towing an empty fuel trailer; this happened to run over a bump as the man leapt, catapulting him back on to the rear of the tank. Centurion crews heartily welcomed the demise of the Mono-trailer when it was replaced in 1963 by an additional 100-gallon armoured fuel tank bolted to the rear hull plate.

Mark 5

As noted above, there were persistent demands from Users, both in BAOR and Korea, for the replacement of the coaxial Besa machine gun with the more reliable .30-calibre Browning. As the Browning was also extensively employed throughout NATO as a tank coaxial, the advantages of ammunition standardisation were self-evident. Trials began in January 1953; the Browning was authorised for production vehicles in late 1954, and tanks fitted with the new coaxial machine gun appeared in

BELOW In late 1955 the British Army adopted the M1919 .30in calibre Browning as the co-axial machine gun for Centurion in place of the 7.92mm Besa. This modification changed the designation of Centurion Mark 3 to Mark 5. At the same time a fume extractor was added to the main armament as the 20pdr B Type barrel. A later modification was the welding of extra armour on the glacis plate (shown here) that again changed the designation to Centurion Mark 5/1.

the summer of 1955 under the designation Centurion Mark 5. The first unit to receive them was the demonstration squadron of 1RTR at the School of Infantry, Warminster, that September. Apart from the different cradle and mounting, Centurion Mark 5 was identical to the Mark 3. During late 1955 and 1956 all Centurions Mark 3 were retrospectively fitted with the Browning coaxial machine gun and became Mark 5s. From May 1957 an additional Browning was fitted to the commander's cupola of Centurion gun tanks for ground and air defence.

Meanwhile, far-reaching changes were in hand as new design features were being developed at FVRDE. Among these were a new type of gun mantlet embodying resiliently mounted trunnions, whereby impact from a direct hit would be absorbed to reduce the possibility of the trunnions shearing; improved gun elevation gear, to provide simpler installation with more efficient and accurate

CENTRE Experience in BAOR, Egypt and Korea led to the development of an improved Centurion in 1952. The most pressing problem of limited range was addressed by the addition of a 95-gallon fuel tank underneath armour in an enlarged rear hull, designated Centurion Mark 7. This view shows the connection boxes for the Mono-trailer, the deeper mud and dust guards at the rear, and the revised towing hook.

RIGHT 42BA43 is an early production Mark 7 with an A Type 20-pounder gun barrel and the earlier bazooka plates with fewer camouflage garnishing hooks. Because of the additional rear fuel tank for the Mark 7 it was necessary to revise the cooling air outlet system so 'pagoda type' louvres were incorporated on both the engine and transmission compartment covers.

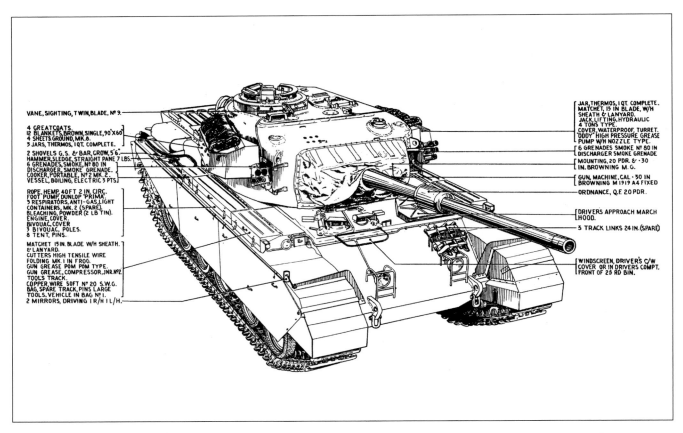

VANE, SIGHTING, TWIN, BLADE, Nº 9.

4 GREATCOATS.
12 BLANKETS, BROWN, SINGLE, 90"X60"
4 SHEETS GROUND, MK.8.
5 JARS, THERMOS, 1QT. COMPLETE.

2 SHOVELS G.S. & BAR, CROW, 5'6".
HAMMER, SLEDGE, STRAIGHT PANE 7 LBS.
6 GRENADES, SMOKE, Nº 80 IN
DISCHARGER, SMOKE, GRENADE.
COOKER, PORTABLE (2 LB TIN).
VESSEL, BOILING, ELECTRIC 3 PTS.

ROPE, HEMP, 40 FT 2 IN. CIRC.
FOOT PUMP, DUNLOP "PRIMA".
5 RESPIRATORS, ANTI-GAS, LIGHT
CONTAINERS, MK. 2 (SPARE).
BLEACHING, POWDER (2 LB TIN).
ENGINE, COVER.
BIVOUAC, COVER.
3 BIVOUAC, POLES.
8 TENT, PINS.

MATCHET 15 IN. BLADE W/H SHEATH.
& LANYARD.
CUTTERS HIGH TENSILE WIRE
FOLDING MK. 1 IN. FROG.
GUN GREASE POM POM TYPE.
GUN GREASE, COMPRESSOR, JNR.Nº2.
TOOLS TRACK.
COPPER, WIRE SOFT Nº 20 S.W.G.
BAG, SPARE TRACK, PINS LARGE
TOOLS, VEHICLE IN BAG Nº 1.
2 MIRRORS, DRIVING 1 R/H 1 L/H.

JAR, THERMOS, 1 QT. COMPLETE.
MATCHET, 15 IN BLADE, W/H
SHEATH & LANYARD.
JACK, LIFTING, HYDRAULIC
4 TONS TYPE.
COVER, WATERPROOF, TURRET.
'ODDY' HIGH PRESSURE GREASE
PUMP W/H NOZZLE TYPE.
6 GRENADES SMOKE Nº 80 IN
DISCHARGER SMOKE GRENADE
MOUNTING, 20 PDR. & .30
IN. BROWNING M.G.
GUN, MACHINE, CAL .30 IN
BROWNING M 1919 A4 FIXED
ORDNANCE, Q.F. 20 PDR.
DRIVERS APPROACH MARCH
HOOD.
3 TRACK LINKS 24 IN. (SPARE)
WINDSCREEN, DRIVER'S C/W
COVER OR IN DRIVERS COMPT.
FRONT OF 25 RD BIN.

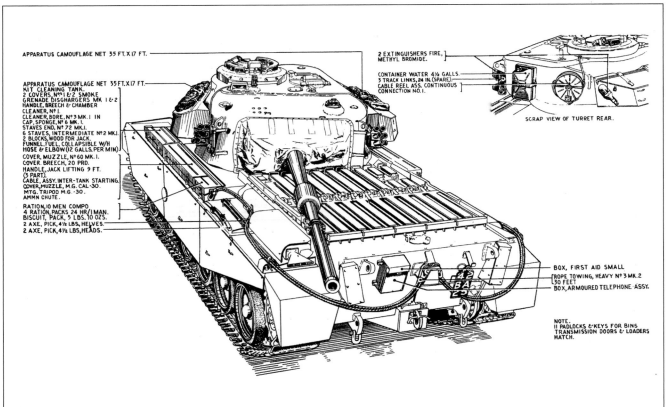

APPARATUS CAMOUFLAGE NET 35 FT. X 17 FT.

APPARATUS CAMOUFLAGE NET 35 FT. X 17 FT.
KIT CLEANING TANK.
2 COVERS, Nº 1 & 2 SMOKE
GRENADE DISGHARGERS MK 1 & 2
HANDLE, BREECH & CHAMBER
CLEANER, Nº 1.
CLEANER, BORE, Nº 3 MK. 1 IN
CAP, SPONGE, Nº 6 MK. 1.
STAVES END, Nº 72 MK.1.
6 STAVES, INTERMEDIATE Nº 2 MK.1.
2 BLOCKS, WOOD FOR JACK.
FUNNEL, FUEL, COLLAPSIBLE W/H
HOSE & ELBOW (12 GALLS. PER MIN)

COVER, MUZZLE, Nº 60 MK.1.
COVER, BREECH, 20 PRD.
HANDLE, JACK LIFTING 9 FT.
(3 PART).
CABLE, ASSY. INTER-TANK STARTING.
COVER, MUZZLE, M.G. CAL .30.
MTG. TRIPOD M.G. .30.
AMMN. CHUTE.

RATION, 10 MEN COMPO
4 RATION, PACKS 24 HR/1 MAN.
BISCUIT, PACK, 5 LBS. 10 OZS.
2 AXE, PICK, 4½ LBS, HELVES.
2 AXE, PICK, 4½ LBS, HEADS.

2 EXTINGUISHERS FIRE,
METHYL BROMIDE.

CONTAINER WATER 4½ GALLS.
3 TRACK LINKS, 24 IN. (SPARE)
CABLE REEL ASS. CONTINUOUS
CONNECTION NO. 1.

SCRAP VIEW OF TURRET REAR.

BOX, FIRST AID SMALL
ROPE TOWING, HEAVY Nº 3 MK.2
30 FEET
BOX, ARMOURED TELEPHONE. ASSY.

NOTE.
11 PADLOCKS & KEYS FOR BINS
TRANSMISSION DOORS & LOADERS
HATCH.

operation; improved ventilation and dispersal of gun fumes; an emergency gun firing set in case of failure of the main system; a more reliable turret sealing ring and improvements to auxiliary engine, generator and fan drive.

In January 1952 it was decided to introduce another mark of vehicle embodying an entirely new internal arrangement including all past and present modifications and those design improvements that could be readily incorporated. Design parentage of the new vehicle was entrusted to Leyland Motors, who submitted the design specification of Centurion Mark 7 on 10 October 1952. The Mark 6 designation was reserved for a conversion of existing Centurions when a new tank gun in the process of being designed became available.

Mark 7

The new features of the proposed Mark 7 were as follows:

- an extended hull to accommodate an additional 95-gallon fuel tank under armour in the rear
- lighter 'pagoda type' air louvres on engine and transmission decks
- a turret turntable with rotating floor
- a new electrical system
- improved ammunition stowage with more 'ready' rounds accessible
- ammunition loading port in left hull side
- larger fuel fillers, relocated to avoid having to traverse the turret when refuelling
- a longer-life exhaust system
- minor improvements in controls, sights, seating, stowage and so on
- the latest type of gun-control equipment (FVGCE No 1 Mark 6), marked in mils instead of degrees and minutes
- charging set engine controls in the driver's

compartment
- commander's elevation hand control gear (on previous vehicles only an overriding traverse control was provided)
- new cupola with overhead protection and UNF (unified screw threads) to conform with American National standard.

In November 1952, a mock-up of the vehicle was inspected and approved by the Users' Committee. The design was sealed at this stage, although the new cupola and gun mounting were still under development. As extensive proving trials of these items were still to be conducted, it was decided to incorporate these later in order to allow production of Centurion Mark 7 to proceed. By the end of 1953 production of components was under way, and Mark 7s were built at a new Ministry of Supply factory in Leyland, Lancashire, at ROF Barnbow and at Vickers-Armstrongs.

Development efforts were now concentrated on clearance of the outstanding design features, and a new model of Meteor engine with mechanically instead of belt-driven fans.

BELOW From the front the principal visual difference of the Mark 7 was the revised headlights that now conformed to civilian standards. This necessitated the relocation of the spare track links and of the driver's approach march hood stowage bin. Again the track guards have been extended downwards to reduce the amount of dust or mud thrown up during travel.

OPPOSITE TOP Centurion Mark 7, stowage sketch exterior, front and right side

OPPOSITE BOTTOM Centurion Mark 7, stowage sketch exterior, rear and left side.

Furthermore, a War Office requirement for additional frontal armour protection had been made, and it was planned to introduce these items on a new mark of vehicle as well as the many modifications approved since the Centurion Mark 7 programme began. However, only 12 of the new Meteor Mark 4C engines were built for trials purposes, and although this version had double the life of the Mark 4B it was not introduced in any production Centurion for various reasons, the most important being the trend towards multi-fuel engines.

Mark 8

The new gun mounting was ready in July 1955 and the first prototype vehicle incorporating the resilient mounting was delivered in September. The production programme of Centurion Mark 8 was authorised that November, and although basically similar to its predecessors it had many new features. The turret front and roof were redesigned to accommodate the resilient gun mounting, and the new commander's cupola No 4 Mark 1 with the RCP sight and ×10 binoculars adjacent was introduced. The cupola had the facility of 'contra-rotation' to assist in target acquisition, by enabling the commander to lay the gun on a target without interrupting his observation of it. The cupola also incorporated two semi-circular hatch doors, which could be raised in the closed position to give 'umbrella' protection while retaining the advantages of direct vision; they were also lighter than the previous type and considerably easier to open. The gun elevating

BELOW Production of the Centurion Mark 8 began in November 1955 and introduced several new features, including a resiliently mounted mantlet for the main armament (seen here); a new cupola No 4 Mark 1; revised gun elevating gear and the latest gun control equipment.

gear was revised, with a gun cradle-mounted gearbox to simplify production and installation. Gun elevation was achieved by chain drive instead of gears, but was not as smooth for gun laying and required more maintenance. The latest gun control equipment (FVGCE No 1 Mark 8) was fitted with an electrical instead of a manual changeover from hand to stabilised control. A velocity-sensitive control automatically engaged the stabiliser system when the alternator and metadyne were switched on and the tank exceed a speed of 1.5mph.

User trials of Centurion Mark 8 were conducted in BAOR by 3rd Dragoon Guards and 4th/7th Dragoon Guards in late 1956. Trials were also carried out in November 1956 of a Mark 8 (45BA11) fitted with additional frontal armour in the form of a 1.7in-thick appliqué patch welded to the glacis plate. As there were no adverse effects on performance, riding characteristics, range or maintenance requirements, the additional armour was authorised for production vehicles and all Mark 8s except for the first 28 were uparmoured during manufacture. In this way the armour thickness of the glacis plate was increased to 5in (126mm), thus proof against the 100mm APHE round of the Soviet T54/55 series at normal combat ranges. This policy was extended to include most Centurion gun tanks in the British Army, and Marks 5, 7 and remaining 8s were uparmoured during base overhaul from January 1959 onwards. When the additional armour was fitted, the vehicle designation altered: for instance, an uparmoured Mark 5 became Centurion Mark 5/1, and this also applied to the other marks.

The L7 gun

In the meantime, development of tank guns and ammunition had proceeded apace. An outline specification was prepared in July 1956 for a 105mm high-velocity gun to fit the breech and gun mounting of the existing 20-pounder.

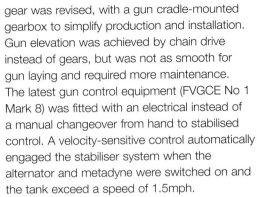

BELOW Production of the Centurion Mark 8 began in November 1955 and introduced several new features, including a resiliently mounted mantlet for the main armament (seen here); a new cupola No 4 Mark 1; revised gun elevating gear and the latest gun control equipment.

OPPOSITE TOP Centurion Mark 7, plan view.

OPPOSITE BOTTOM Centurion Mark 7, stowage sketch interior, turret front and left side.

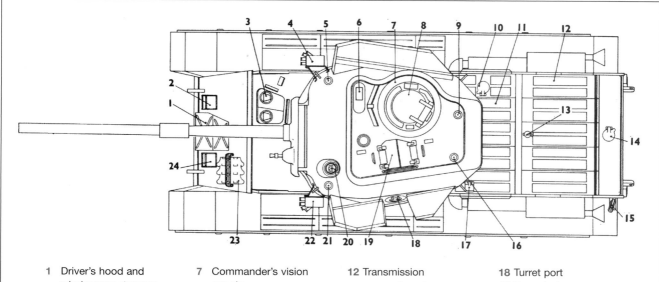

1 Driver's hood and windscreen stowage bin	7 Commander's vision cupola	12 Transmission compartment covers	18 Turret port
2 Headlamp	8 Commander's access door	13 Coolant filler access	19 Operator's access doors
3 Driver's access doors	9 Aerial base	14 Rear fuel filler access	20 Operator's periscope
4 Smoke dischargers	10 Right-hand fuel filler access	15 Gun crutch	21 Aerial base
5 Aerial base	11 Engine compartment covers	16 Aerial base	22 Smoke dischargers
6 Gunner's sighting periscope		17 Charging set oil filler access	23 Spare track links
			24 Headlamp

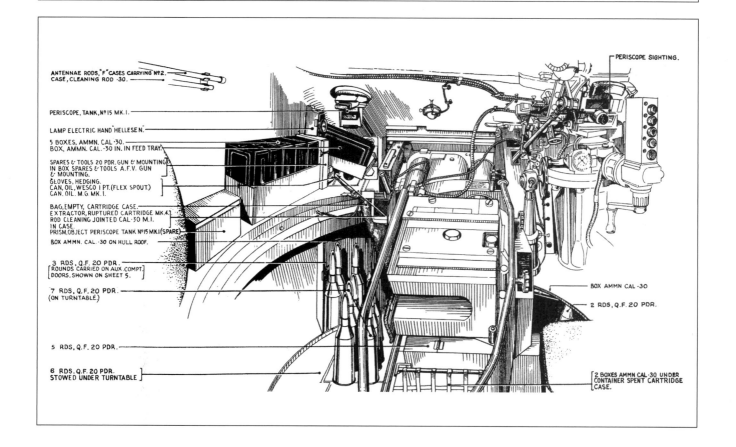

ANTENNAE RODS, "F" CASES CARRYING Nº2.
CASE, CLEANING ROD ·30.

PERISCOPE, TANK, Nº 15 MK.1.

LAMP ELECTRIC HAND HELLESEN.

5 BOXES, AMMN. CAL ·30.
BOX, AMMN. CAL. ·30 IN. IN FEED TRAY.

SPARES & TOOLS 20 PDR. GUN & MOUNTING
IN BOX SPARES & TOOLS A.F.V. GUN
& MOUNTING.
GLOVES, HEDGING.
CAN, OIL, WESCO 1 PT. (FLEX SPOUT.)
CAN, OIL, M.G. MK.1.

BAG, EMPTY, CARTRIDGE CASE.
EXTRACTOR, RUPTURED CARTRIDGE MK.4.
ROD CLEANING JOINTED CAL ·30 M.I.
IN CASE.
PRISM, OBJECT PERISCOPE TANK Nº 15 MK.1 (SPARE)
BOX AMMN. CAL. ·30 ON HULL ROOF.

3 RDS. Q.F. 20 PDR.
[ROUNDS CARRIED ON AUX. COMPT.]
[DOORS, SHOWN ON SHEET 5.]

7 RDS. Q.F. 20 PDR.
(ON TURNTABLE.)

5 RDS. Q.F. 20 PDR.

6 RDS. Q.F. 20 PDR.
STOWED UNDER TURNTABLE.

PERISCOPE SIGHTING.

BOX AMMN CAL ·30

2 RDS. Q.F. 20 PDR.

2 BOXES AMMN CAL ·30 UNDER
CONTAINER SPENT CARTRIDGE
CASE.

RIGHT 91BA51 was a Centurion Mark 9 of the Gunnery Wing at Lulworth. The Mark 9 was uparmoured and rearmed with the outstanding L7 105mm gun, which became the standard tank weapon for much of the NATO alliance during the 1960s and onwards. In the hands of experienced gunnery instructors a Centurion with 105mm was capable of engaging and hitting ten different targets within one minute.

The Hungarian uprising of November 1956 gave Western designers a rare opportunity to determine the threat of potential enemy equipment when patriots drove a captured Soviet T54 into the grounds of the British Embassy, though the military attaché's staff had but a brief time to inspect the tank before it was deemed politic to remove it from the premises. The armour thickness of the glacis plate was erroneously measured as 120mm at 60 degrees (it is in fact 100mm). Accordingly, the performance of the 105mm gun was required to defeat such a thickness of armour at 1,000yd. Comparative firing trials were held between the 105mm, 20-pounder and American 120mm L1A1.

The 105mm gun exceeded the stated requirement with ease, demonstrating 22% greater penetrating ability than the 20-pounder. Following the success of these preliminary trials, a vehicle was converted at FVRDE to carry the new gun and ammunition, the latter still in mock-up form. The two types of ammunition, APDS and HE, determined the ammunition stowage layout. The HE round was some 2.5in longer and 5lb heavier than the 20-pounder shell. Despite this disadvantage, by further limitation of operating space a total stowage of 70 rounds was achieved as compared with 63 rounds on Centurion Mark 7 and 65 on Centurion Marks 3 and 5. Design of the L7 105mm gun was undertaken at the Royal Armament Research and Development Establishment, Fort Halstead. It was more closely integrated with vehicle design requirements, and consequently the fume extractor was mounted eccentrically to allow greater gun depression over the

rear decks. This also enabled simpler gun depression stop rails to be developed; these were extruded-section rubber rails instead of moulded blocks, with a cost saving of 75%. Despite its proven superiority of firepower, there was no service requirement for the L7 105mm gun, so a production licence was offered to Vickers Limited, who made the initial batch of guns. This has given rise to the oft-quoted but erroneous designation of Vickers L7 105mm gun. Due to the insistence of Major General H. Foote VC, then Director of the Royal Armoured Corps, authority was obtained in February 1958 to procure the 105mm gun for the British Army, and production was assigned to ROFs Cardiff and Nottingham.

Marks 9 and 10

A single Centurion (42BA34) was built in 1959 incorporating the gun on an uparmoured Mark 7 chassis under the designation Centurion Mark 9. This vehicle was not put into series production, but the War Office ordered more than 200 sets of conversion equipment to the original FVRDE drawings, thus enabling Royal Electrical and Mechanical Engineers (REME) workshops to convert Centurions Mark 7 to Mark 9. As a natural sequence, the 105mm gun and

OPPOSITE TOP Centurion Mark 7, stowage sketch interior, turret rear and right side.

OPPOSITE BOTTOM Centurion Mark 7, stowage sketch interior, ammunition stowage and driver's compartment

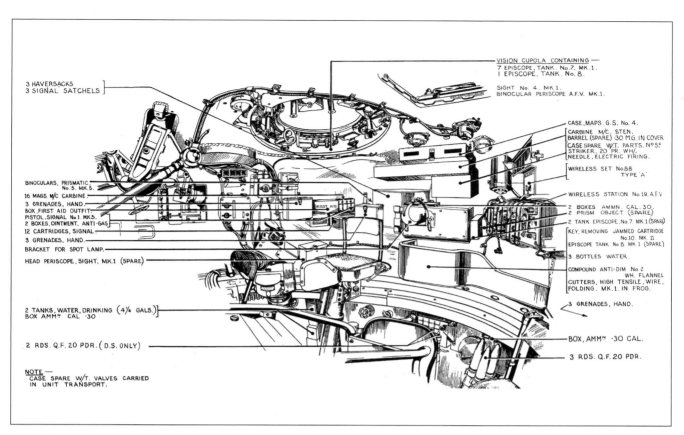

VISION CUPOLA CONTAINING —
7 EPISCOPE, TANK. No.7. MK.1.
1 EPISCOPE, TANK. No. 8.

SIGHT No. 4. MK.1.
BINOCULAR PERISCOPE A.F.V. MK.1.

3 HAVERSACKS
3 SIGNAL SATCHELS

CASE, MAPS, G.S. No. 4.
CARBINE M/C. STEN.
BARREL (SPARE) .30 M.G. IN COVER
CASE SPARE W/T. PARTS. No.55
STRIKER, 20 PR. WH/.
NEEDLE, ELECTRIC FIRING.

WIRELESS SET No.88
TYPE 'A'

BINOCULARS, PRISMATIC
No. 5. MK. 5.
16 MAGS. M/C CARBINE
3 GRENADES, HAND.
BOX, FIRST AID OUTFIT.
PISTOL, SIGNAL No.1. MK.5.
2 BOXES, OINTMENT, ANTI-GAS.
12 CARTRIDGES, SIGNAL.
3 GRENADES, HAND.
BRACKET FOR SPOT LAMP.
HEAD PERISCOPE, SIGHT, MK.1. (SPARE)

WIRELESS STATION No.19. A.F.V.
2 BOXES AMMN. CAL. 30.
2 PRISM OBJECT (SPARE).
2 TANK EPISCOPE, No.7, MK.1. (SPARE)
KEY, REMOVING JAMMED CARTRIDGE
No.10. MK. 11
EPISCOPE, TANK No 8. MK 1 (SPARE)
3 BOTTLES WATER.
COMPOUND ANTI-DIM No.2
WH. FLANNEL
CUTTERS, HIGH TENSILE, WIRE,
FOLDING, MK.1. IN FROG.

2 TANKS, WATER, DRINKING (4¼ GALS.)
BOX AMMN. CAL .30

3 GRENADES, HAND.

2 RDS. Q.F. 20 PDR. (D.S. ONLY)

BOX, AMMN. .30 CAL.

3 RDS. Q.F. 20 PDR.

NOTE —
CASE SPARE W/T. VALVES CARRIED
IN UNIT TRANSPORT.

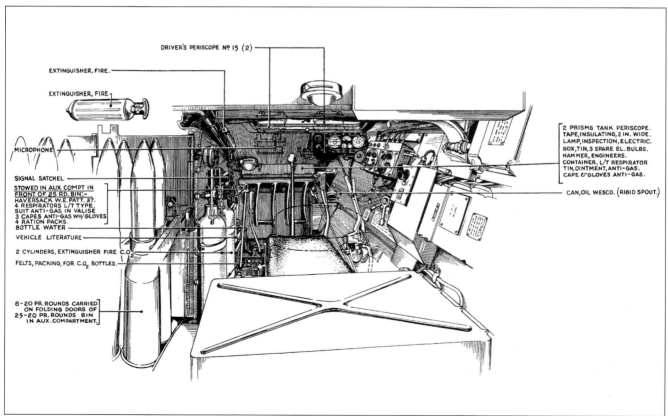

DRIVER'S PERISCOPE No 15 (2)

EXTINGUISHER, FIRE.

EXTINGUISHER, FIRE.

2. PRISMS TANK PERISCOPE.
TAPE, INSULATING, 2 IN. WIDE.
LAMP, INSPECTION, ELECTRIC.
BOX, TIN, 3 SPARE EL. BULBS.
HAMMER, ENGINEERS.
CONTAINER, L/T RESPIRATOR
TIN, OINTMENT, ANTI-GAS.
CAPE & GLOVES ANTI-GAS.

MICROPHONE

CAN, OIL WESCO. (RIGID SPOUT.)

SIGNAL SATCHEL
STOWED IN AUX COMPT IN
FRONT OF 25 RD. BIN:-
HAVERSACK W.E. PATT. 37.
4 RESPIRATORS L/T TYPE.
SUIT ANTI-GAS IN VALISE
3 CAPES ANTI-GAS WH/ GLOVES
4 RATION PACKS.
BOTTLE WATER

VEHICLE LITERATURE

2 CYLINDERS, EXTINGUISHER FIRE C.O.

FELTS, PACKING, FOR C.O₂ BOTTLES.

8 - 20 PR. ROUNDS CARRIED
ON FOLDING DOORS OF
25-20 PR. ROUNDS BIN
IN AUX. COMPARTMENT.

ammunition were also applied to Centurion Mark 8, thus giving rise to Centurion Mark 10. User trials of the 105mm gun began in BAOR on 15 July 1959 at Hohne gunnery ranges, Firing Point 7B, conducted by 4th/7th Dragoon Guards. Two Centurion Mark 8s (44BA81 and 45BA89), converted at 7th Armoured Workshops with L7A1 105mm guns, were extensively tested and the gun was enthusiastically accepted into service.

Production of Centurion Mark 10 began in 1959 and the first vehicles were completed in early 1960. Several suspension modifications were incorporated to give improved spring and guide rod locking. A new design of final drive-bearing minimised the risk of overloading and failure due to unforeseen shock loads; when unloading from a tank transporter, the tank's weight transferred to the sprocket and rear suspension unit as it reversed down the ramps, placing an inordinate strain on those components. These modifications were also incorporated in existing vehicles. The only visible identifying features of late production new-build Centurions Mark 10 were the revised engine louvres of the chevron type, which gave better immunity against shell bursts and improved cooling performance, and were 20% lighter than the 'pagoda' type to enable easier handling. The Mark 10 was the final production model of the Centurion, and the last Centurion gun tank (03DA03) was completed at ROF Barnbow on 30 March 1962.

BELOW Mark 10 Centurions of 1 RTR manoeuvre on the gunnery ranges near Little Aden in 1966. The tanks are painted in a camouflage scheme of black stripes over sand stone colour. The white stripe down the bazooka plate indicates the Amphibious Warfare Squadron (AWS), which remained afloat on Tank Landing Ships to be deployed at short notice to any trouble spots in the region, particularly the Persian Gulf.

Later marks

With production of the 105mm gun well advanced, sufficient weapons became available to institute an upgunning programme for earlier marks of Centurion. The modification itself was straightforward enough and, besides the replacement of the 20-pounder barrel, entailed the installation of new buffer lugs, ammunition racks and clips, gun depression rail, cartridge case deflector, sight scales and barrel-cleaning equipment, plus a modification to the gun crutch. Vehicle designations altered as a result of this modification, depending on the state of the vehicle before conversion. Thus a Mark 5 in its original configuration became, with the addition of the 105mm gun, a Mark 5/2, whereas an uparmoured Mark 5/1 with 105mm gun advanced the designation to Mark 6. This also applied to Mark 7s, which became either Mark 7/2 or Mark 9. As the majority of Mark 8s had been uparmoured during production and were therefore Mark 8/1s *ab initio*, they became Mark 10s. By this time all the original 28 Mark 8s had been uparmoured to Mark 8/1 standard, and they advanced to Mark 10 as well. The designation Mark 8/2 for an original Mark 8 with 105mm gun therefore did not apply in practice. In fact there were very few Centurion Mark 5/2s or Mark 7/2s in service with the British Army, as those tanks that had not been uparmoured before conversion with 105mm guns had both modifications carried out simultaneously during base overhaul. The upgunning programme began in March 1962.

The next major modification programme was the introduction of infrared (IR) night driving and fighting equipment. Trials of a Philips system were conducted in February and March 1960. Infrared illumination for the gunner and commander was provided by a 22in 1kW IR searchlight mounted on the mantlet and aligned along the main armament line-of-sight, while IR periscopes were provided to replace the normal gunner's and commander's periscopes. The previous two centrally mounted driving lights were replaced with four headlights mounted in pairs at either side of the glacis plate with IR lights outermost. These lights were fitted with detachable IR filters, as was the searchlight. The introduction of IR equipment

imposed an increased load on the vehicle's electrical system, requiring modifications to the existing vehicle charging system as well as the installation of two further 12V batteries in the hull. The equipment proved adequate for the task, and it was possible to acquire a live stationary target (*ie*, one emitting an infrared signature such as a vehicle) at 500yd. Positive identification occurred at 250yd, but the ranges increased if the vehicle under observation was moving. Weather and atmospheric conditions had a significant bearing on performance, since rain or mist degraded the image considerably.

The limitation of such a system was that any tank using an infrared projector in the active mode was readily visible to an enemy equipped with similar apparatus. The facility for passive use was therefore tactically more important, and it was in this role that it was normally employed. One of the shortcomings of Centurion was that, with its external exhaust pipes, it had a high IR signature (indeed, at night it was often possible to see the glow of hot exhaust pipes with the naked eye). Installation of infrared equipment began in 1965, and consequently vehicle designations were altered once again: Centurion Mark 6 became Mark 6/1 and Marks 9 and 10 became 9/1 and 10/1.

The final modification programme of any significance was the installation of the 0.50in ranging machine gun in 1966. This system offered a simple and accurate method of

ABOVE The next significant modifications after rearming with the L7 105mm gun was the introduction of IR night-fighting equipment and ranging gun to enhance range estimation on the battlefield (the cause of most gunnery errors). The device comprised a .50-calibre Browning mounted coaxially with the main armament in the mantlet and aligned precisely with the gunner's sights.

rangefinding as opposed to complex optical instruments. It was potentially superior to optical rangefinders because of its ability to provide additionally the lateral aim-off for factors such as trunnion tilt, crosswinds and drift, and also to compensate for changes in ambient

LEFT The British Army was slow to adopt infrared (IR) night-fighting equipment for tanks after the war. In the early 1960s an IR system developed by Philips was adopted for Centurion incorporating night viewing for the driver via a second pair of headlights on the glacis plate, and a 22in searchlight (shown here) in the stowage basket at the rear of the turret when not mounted on the mantlet.

RIGHT AND BELOW
The ultimate model of Centurion in British Army service was the Mark 13 that originated as either a Mark 8 or 10 and was progressively modified with many improvements, notably IR night-fighting equipment, ranging gun and a thermal sleeve for the 105mm gun to minimise barrel distortion due to extended firing or climatic conditions.

temperatures. It was particularly advantageous when used with medium-velocity ammunition such as the High-Explosive Squash Head (HESH) round introduced for the 105mm gun in 1960.

The ranging gun itself was a modified .50-calibre M2 Browning (L21) mounted coaxially in the mantlet. It fired three-round bursts of incendiary-tipped tracer ammunition, which ignited on striking a hard object. By observing the fall of bullets at a determined range until they struck the target, the reading was then transferred to the chosen ammunition scale of the main armament, and the gun fired. At ranges above 1,000yd this method was faster than shell ranging, with an average engagement time of 15 seconds. The use of a ranging gun did not disclose the tank's position to the extent one might expect, and observation of the tracer rounds was possible in any light conditions except when they were so bad that targets could not be acquired anyway.

However, in British service the ranging-gun mounting proved somewhat unreliable, leading on occasions to inconsistent and misleading range data. The Dutch Army developed a different mounting for their Centurions with markedly superior results. This problem, together with the fact that observation of the fall of bullets in broken, undulating ground or wooded areas was difficult, led to reservations as to its value. Be that as it may, the ranging gun was a practical alternative to the optical rangefinders of the period; in fact, until the introduction of lasers there was no really effective rapid method of ranging for tanks. Within the limitations of the era, the ranging gun was as good a system as any.

At the same time as the installation of ranging guns, a thermal sleeve was fitted to the main gun barrel to prevent distortion caused by solar energy, wind, rain and abrupt temperature changes. (It was also a useful indicator that a ranging gun was fitted.) If the thermal sleeve was not fitted for any reason, a further identification point was that the barrel was painted black instead of green; the black paint gave a more even dissipation of heat and enhanced the effectiveness of the thermal sleeve.

This installation of ranging guns on Centurions changed the vehicle designation yet again and produced the final marks of the series. A standard Mark 6 with ranging gun became Mark 6/2, and it altered Mark 9 to 9/2 and Mark 10 to 10/2. Those tanks that had already been fitted with IR equipment – Marks 6/1, 9/1 and 10/1 – became Marks 11, 12 and 13 respectively. As a corollary, Centurions Mark 6/2, 9/2 and 10/2, when subsequently fitted with IR equipment, became Marks 11, 12 and 13. There were therefore 24 marks and sub-marks of Centurion gun tanks, excluding A41 and the 'paper' designations of Centurion Mark 4 and Mark 8/2.

Centurion production

Centurion was built at three separate production lines. Mark 1 was produced at ROFs Barnbow, Nottingham and Woolwich Arsenal; Marks 2, 3 and 5 at ROF Barnbow and Vickers-Armstrongs; Marks 7 and 8 at ROF Barnbow and Leyland Motors, and Mark 10 at ROF Barnbow, Leeds.

An analysis of the weight of Centurion shows that 44% of it comprised armour, 11% armament and ammunition, 5% powerplant,

RIGHT A Centurion hull is fabricated in a manipulator that allowed all welds to be made from above thereby improving the strength and integrity of the joints. Production was undertaken on two assembly lines running in parallel; one for the hulls and one for the turrets.

ABOVE On 22 July 1974, when the last Centurion gun tank was withdrawn from service with the Royal Armoured Corps, the occasion was marked with a final salvo on the gunnery range at Lulworth. Centurion Mark 13, 04CC87, was manned by some venerable veterans of Centurion with Colonel Eric Offord in the background, Lieutenant Colonel Ken Hill (right), Major Bert Starr in the commander's cupola, and Major Dai Mitchell in the driver's seat.

30% transmission and running gear and 10% for crew, stowage and ancillaries. At the height of production in 1953 Centurions were built at the rate of 11 per week and assembly took approximately three months. The cost of a Centurion in 1951 was £38,000, of which £1,600 was for the gun control equipment.

A large number of Centurions were exported, and overseas customers included Australia,

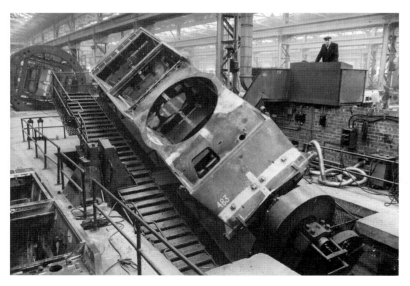

LEFT The holes for the gun trunnions are drilled through the front face of the turret: a procedure that requires absolute accuracy to seat the gun cradle properly. This is a mid-production turret with the loader's periscope situated on the forward part of the turret roof.

CENTRE With its 20-pounder gun the completed turret is prepared for mounting on a hull. The only item that was not fitted at the factory was the coaxial machine gun since it was deemed to be too prone to theft.

Canada, Denmark, Egypt, Holland, India, Iraq, Israel, Kuwait, New Zealand, South Africa, Sweden and Switzerland. It must be stated that a measure of its sales success was due to the lack of competition in the early 1950s as the only nations building tanks in quantity were Great Britain, the USA and USSR. Be that as it may, foreign sales of new-built vehicles exceeded £200 million. A further £600 million was realised for ammunition for these tanks. Considerable further monies came from the sale of second-hand vehicles to Israel and elsewhere, and the continuing sales of spare parts and ammunition increased the total still more. This can be considered a satisfactory return on the development cost of Centurion, which did not exceed £5 million.

Foreign upgrades

It is indicative of the sound basic design of Centurion that, in British Army service, it was uparmoured once and upgunned twice, finally mounting the outstanding L7A1 105mm gun. This weapon has been further enhanced by improved types of ammunition and it remains in service as a potent main armament for tanks to this day. In November 1966, the Chieftain main battle tank began to replace Centurion in the armoured regiments of the British Army.

LEFT Turret and hull of a Centurion Mark 3 are married in the final stages of assembly. This is a mid-production turret as the rear hatch had been eliminated since the 20-pounder gun was replaced from the front.

ABOVE AND BELOW Following the Six-Day War of June 1967, the Israeli Armored Corps embarked on a major programme to rectify the problems associated with Centurion during the conflict, in particular its high fuel consumption and limited operating range. The solution was found in replacing the Meteor engine with the same power pack as used on the Magach (M48A3 version) that was also in service to provide commonality across the fleet. The power pack comprised the Teledyne Continental AVDS-1790-2A air-cooled diesel engine and the Allison CD-850-6 automatic transmission. This combination provided greater performance, reliability, range and much simpler driving. To differentiate between the two types of Centurion that was named Shot or Whip in IDF service, the petrol-engined Centurion was known as Shot Meteor and the upgraded version Shot Cal, Cal signifying Continental and not Kal, which means 'light' – as in weight – in Hebrew, and Centurion could never be termed light. Shown above is the Shot Meteor and below the Shot Cal on comparative trials in the Negev Desert.

LEFT In the 1970s and '80s there was a thriving market to upgrade earlier generation battle tanks. Vickers Limited offered the Centurion Retrofit, with a range of improvements depending on the requirements and budget of the purchaser, primarily to replace the obsolescent Meteor engine and Merritt-Brown gearbox with an integral power pack. Upgunning and uparmouring was also available as well as an NBC ventilation system. This Centurion Retrofit model was tested by the Swiss Army but was passed over in favour of procurement of Leopard 2.

BELOW The most important improvement was a diesel V800 power pack comprising a 12V-71T V12 turbo-charged engine combined with a TN12 semi- or fully automatic six-speed gearbox as used in Chieftain for greater automotive performance, reliability and reduced operational costs. When combined with modified final drives this combination gave an output of 715bhp with a maximum speed of 25mph and a much enhanced operational range.

Surplus Centurions were then sold with the majority being purchased by the Israel Defense Forces (IDF) at an average price of £10,000 per tank. The Centurion, designated 'Shot', the Hebrew word for whip or scourge, in IDF service proved highly successful during the Six-Day War of June 1967 when the Israeli Armored Corps possessed 338 Centurions. However, during the rapid advance across the Sinai Desert, the high fuel consumption of the Meteor petrol engine caused logistical nightmares. Immediately after the war, an upgrade programme was initiated by General Israel Tal to rectify the problem. Various engines were tested but the Teledyne Continental AVDS-1790-2A air-cooled diesel engine was selected both for its better performance and fuel consumption and also because this power plant powered the later models of the M48 Magach to give greater commonality across the tank fleet. The Shot Cal was accepted for service on 5 May 1970 (Cal referring to Continental, while those still fitted with the petrol engine were called Shot Meteor).

At the same time the Royal Netherlands Army produced a similar upgraded Centurion employing the same Continental engine coupled to an Allison CD-850-6 automatic transmission. After trials lasting six months, the scheme was abandoned in favour of the procurement of the German Leopard 1. Throughout the 1970s and into the 1980s, there were various Centurion upgrade programmes offered, from Krauss Maffei to Vickers, for a worldwide market that comprised some 2,800 Centurion battle tanks. All offered a main armament upgrade, invariably the L7A1 105mm gun, with an enhanced fire control system, a new diesel-engine power pack and increased armour protection as required.

Vickers Limited offered the 'Centurion Retrofit' that was powered by a Detroit Diesel 12V71T 720bhp diesel power pack coupled to the David Brown TN12 semi-automatic transmission as used in Chieftain MBT; the L7A1 105mm gun with a fire control system of the client's choice with either a 0.50in-calibre ranging gun or the tank laser sight as fitted to Chieftain. The latter's commander's cupola was an option as was NBC protection and passive night vision equipment. Two versions of this model were purchased by Switzerland and tested between 1973 and 1977 but the retrofit programme was not adopted in quantity. Instead the Swiss investigated the upgrade programme offered by NIMDA and Israel Military Industries.

Based on their wide combat experience, the Israeli version reflected their current model of Shot then in service with the IDF. Although

trialled in Switzerland, it was the Swedish Army that modified its Centurion fleet to this standard, together with a Bofors Aerotronics fire control system incorporating a laser rangefinder. With the characteristic 'Tal Cupola', the upgraded Centurion designated Stridsvagn 104 (Strv104) incorporated a twin 71mm illuminating mortar, a passive night driving periscope for the driver and night vision goggles for the commander. Subsequent improvements included enhanced night vision equipment; modified gun stabilisation; a thermal sleeve and muzzle reference system for the 105mm gun and appliqué reactive armour from FFV Ordnance. A Strv104 of this specification is currently on display at The Tank Museum, Bovington.

The Israeli-upgraded Centurion has also been sold to Singapore and it has become the de facto model on the international market. For those customers that did not wish to trade with Israel, Teledyne Continental Motors (TCM – now owned by the Aviation Industry

BELOW With the installation of the L7 105mm gun the customer was given the option of a .50in-calibre ranging gun, or a fully electronic Gun Control Equipment incorporating a laser rangefinder integrated into the gunner's sight with a digital range read-out for the commander with an accuracy of + or -10m at 10km. The commander in turn was offered a new cupola based on Chieftain with minimal reworking of the roof plate.

began selling arms in quantity to other (then) world pariahs such as Chile, Taiwan and South Africa. During the late 1970s, the latter was in desperate need of modern weapons for use in its extended war in Angola and South West Africa (now Namibia). South Africa was willing to underwrite the development costs of various weapon systems from small arms to nuclear missiles. Since the South African Defence Force was equipped with elderly and increasingly unreliable Centurions due to the embargo on spare parts, it was logical to upgrade them to the IDF Shot Cal specification.

Designated 'Olifant', the Afrikaans word for elephant, the first prototype was produced in 1973 with production beginning in 1978 with 153 Olifants Mark 1 manufactured by 1984. An improved version, the Mark 1A, appeared in 1985 with 79 being built as well as 16 ARVs. In 1987, the Olifant was deployed to Angola for its combat debut where it proved far superior to the T54/55 series employed by the Angolans and Cubans. Following the Angolan War, a much improved model designated Olifant Mark 1B was developed using mainly local technology including passive composite armour, torsion bar suspension and an integrated fire control system.

Since attempts to build a completely indigenous main battle tank (MBT) or procure a foreign design from abroad – among those trialled were the Challenger 2E, the tropicalised Leclerc and the Leopard 2A4 – came to nothing, it was decided to upgrade the Olifant further to become the Olifant Mark 2. Together with an enhanced armour package that is proof against 125mm APFSDS at normal combat ranges over the frontal aspect, the Olifant Mark 2 incorporates a Teledyne Continental power pack producing 1,040bhp and a highly advanced hunter–killer fire control system for the 105mm gun firing the latest Israeli ammunition.

These combined elements have produced a formidable MBT with a fine balance of firepower, mobility and protection: the design prerequisite of Centurion from its inception. For a tank that was accepted into the British Army in 1946, it is quite extraordinary that its ultimate successor should still be in front-line service some 70 years later with no definite retirement date as yet.

ABOVE After the October War of 1973 the Shot Cal was modified to address the threats posed during the conflict, particularly that posed by crew-served and shoulder-fired High Explosive Anti-Tank (HEAT) weapons such as Saggers and RPGs that were employed in profusion by the Egyptians and Syrians. The IDF was among the first to adopt Explosive Reactive Armour (ERA) as a counter-measure to HEAT rounds and the armour array was known as Balan or 'Tiles'.

Corporation of China) offered a similar upgrade package, which was adopted by the Royal Hashemite Kingdom of Jordan. The TCM Jordanian Centurion Modernisation Program was undertaken from 1982 and comprised a reduced-width version of the AVDS 1790-2CC/CD850-6A RISE power pack of the US Army M60 series, combined with a new British Horstmann Hydrostrut suspension system. The package featured a Belgian SABCA Laser Tank Fire Control System and a Delco/Cadillac Gage weapons/Turret Control and Stabilisation system and night vision equipment derived from that on the M60 series. Some 293 Centurions were so converted with the designation of 'Tariq' meaning striker, all armed with the L7 105mm gun.

Much of the Israeli expertise in upgrading armoured fighting vehicles and aircraft was as a consequence of the various arms embargoes imposed on the country by the global community. It was unsurprising then that Israel

ABOVE As revolutionary wars raged across sub-Saharan Africa during the 1970s and '80s, the South African Defence Force increased both its capabilities in counter-insurgency and conventional warfare. With the UN-imposed international arms embargo it was impossible to obtain modern weapons from abroad and so South Africa turned to Israel for expertise and weapons technology. In the field of armour the result was the Olifant (seen here), which bears more than a passing resemblance to the Shot Cal. *(Photograph SAAC)*

RIGHT Several attempts to procure a foreign MBT to replace Olifant included Challenger 2E, Leclerc and Leopard 2A4, but these came to naught. When the threat emerged of the T-72 in southern Africa, it was decided to upgrade the Olifant Mark 1B further still, with the intention of converting all 50 Olifant Mark 1Bs to the new standard. In the event only 26 were reworked to become the Olifant 2, sufficient to equip two squadrons. *(Photograph SAAC)*

Chapter Two

The Centurion Mark 3 in detail

The Centurion Mark 3 was the principal production model with a total of 2,833 being manufactured between 1948 and 1955. Armed with a potent 20-pounder main armament combined with a stabilisation system to ensure accuracy on the move, Centurion was exported in large numbers serving with some 14 armies worldwide.

OPPOSITE HELICON 00ZR94 of 8 RTR, an early production Centurion Mark 3, undertakes driver training on the Yorkshire moors near the garrison town of Catterick. This model incorporated a fully stabilised 20-pounder main armament that allowed the gunner to train on the target while on the move across country. Centurion was the first tank in the world to have such a system.

**Centurion Mark 3 Main
Battle Tank.**

1 Gunner's periscope
2 Sighting vane
3 Commander's cupola
4 Loader's periscope
5 Wireless aerials
6 Camouflage net
7 Stowage bins for
    tools
8 No 80 Smoke
    Grenade Discharger
9 Engine deck
10 Exhaust
11 Stowage bins for
    rations
12 Drive sprocket
13 Roadwheels
14 Bazooka plates
15 Fire extinguisher
    handle
16 Driver's mirror
17 Idler wheel
18 24in-wide tracks
19 Glacis plate
20 Spare track links
21 Towing shackle
22 Driver's folding
    windscreen
23 Driver's periscopes
24 20-pounder main
    armament
25 Muzzle
    counterweight
26 Gun mantlet
27 7.92mm Besa Mk 3
    coaxial machine gun

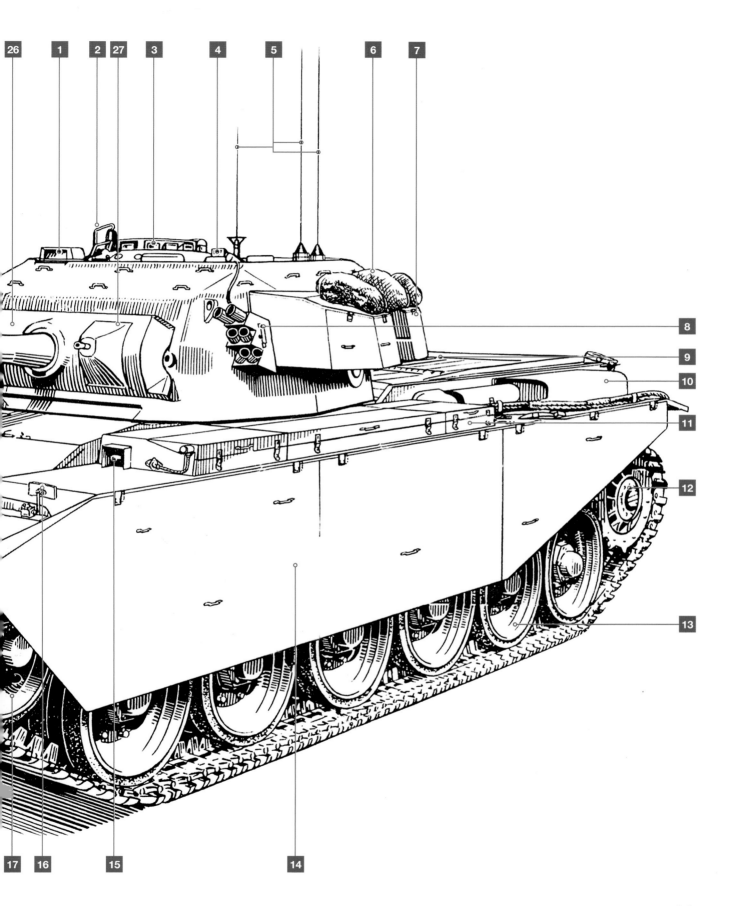

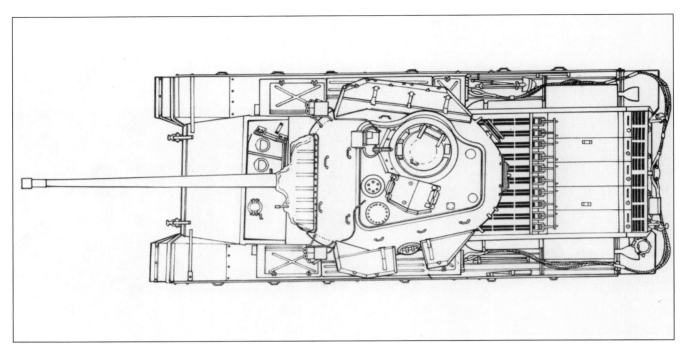

ABOVE **Centurion Mark 3, plan view.**

The first regiment to be fully equipped with Centurion Mark 3 was 1 RTR at Detmold in Germany. Since the Mark 3 was the major production vehicle, it is described below in detail.

The layout was conventional and similar to most tanks of the period. The forward part of the vehicle was divided to form a driver's compartment on the right-hand side and a compartment housing a 20-round ammunition bin and a 10-gallon fresh water tank on the left. The rear of the driver's compartment was open to allow access to the fighting compartment at certain angles of turret traverse. The fighting compartment occupied the centre of the vehicle, accommodating the commander, gunner, loader, main armament and auxiliary weapons, and the bulk of the ammunition. The fighting compartment was separated from the engine compartment by a rear bulkhead which was fitted with a large access plate to facilitate engine maintenance.

LEFT **Driving compartment.**

Behind the Meteor engine was the transmission compartment housing the Merritt-Brown gearbox, cooling fans and steering brakes.

Driving compartment

Access to the compartment was through two interlocking, spring-assisted doors located in the hull top plate. The driver's seat was bolted to the hull floor and was adjustable to one of five positions, four of these for driving when closed down and one when opened up. The seat back could be lowered to an almost horizontal position, to make a most acceptable sleeping arrangement and also to allow the driver to escape through the fighting compartment providing the turret was not traversed between '9 o'clock' and '1 o'clock'. Observation was by means of two No 15 Mark 1 periscopes, one in each of the access hatches. A combined windscreen and hood could be fitted over the driver's hatch to give protection when driving in the opened-up position in bad weather. When not in use, this 'approach-march hood' was stowed in a bin on the left-hand front of the hull in place of one set of spare track links; previous Centurions and early Mark 3s carried the hood in the side stowage bin. A fold-down type of windscreen was provided for driving in the opened position under favourable conditions; this was protected by a canvas cover when not in use and folded down against the hull.

The driving controls consisted of clutch, brake and accelerator arranged left to right, a centrally mounted 2ft 6in gear lever and steering levers on both sides of the seat with the handbrake next to the right-hand lever. To the driver's right were the instrument panel and engine controls, and to his left two CO_2 fire extinguishers. Driving Centurion was no easy task and required both constant concentration and much physical exertion. The tank had five speeds forward and two in reverse; odd numbers were forward in the gear-change gate and even numbers back, with 1st gear on the right and high and low reverses either side of 2nd and 4th; 1st gear was rarely used for moving off except on steep hills, soft ground or when making tight turns. Depressing the heavy clutch required a foot pressure of 60lb, but when in motion it was possible to overcome the inertia of the clutch assembly by pulling lightly

on a steering lever, which served as a clutch stop and allowed rapid gear changes – this was known as a 'stick change'. The driver was thus able to maintain the momentum of the vehicle with minimal loss of speed during gear changes. Across country, an accomplished driver exploiting terrain such as hollows to sustain momentum when changing up could achieve as good or better performance as later semi-automatic or automatic transmissions. To change down it was necessary to double-declutch, and should the driver fail to engage the gear from neutral while climbing hills the result could be dire: the tank might career downhill backwards out of control, and no amount of brake application would stop it as the brake linings burnt out in short order. This idiosyncrasy was well known to Centurion drivers the world over, and each nation had a pithy phrase to describe it, such as 'doing an angel', or 'Mexican overdrive'.

The direction of travel was controlled by the two steering levers which affected the relative speeds of the tracks. Pulling on the left-hand lever reduced the speed of the inner track and by the epicyclic trains speeded the outer, turning the vehicle to the left. As the gearbox gave fixed steering radii according to the gear ratio engaged, it will be readily appreciated that the lower the gear engaged, the sharper would

ABOVE One of the finest exhibits at the Tank Museum is the bisected Centurion that was fabricated by apprentices at ROF Barnbow, Leeds. It graphically conveys the complexity of a battle tank and the cramped conditions endured by the crew. Nevertheless, Centurion was relatively roomy inside and was not an uncomfortable tank to man unlike contemporary Russian designs. This is an important aspect for the efficient running of a tank as adequate space allows the crew to serve their weapons better and just as importantly have room enough to relax when not in action. As with most contemporary designs, Centurion had a four-man crew with three in the turret and the driver in the front hull (opposite left).

be the turn. Thus when the vehicle was moving forward with the higher gears engaged and it became necessary to make a sharp turn, the driver changed down to a lower gear, with a consequential loss of vehicle speed. In reverse the opposite applied and pulling the left-hand steering lever turned the vehicle to the right. One further characteristic of the Merritt-Brown gearbox was that when in neutral steering remained effective while both steering levers were forward and the clutch engaged, so it was possible to achieve a neutral turn when either of the steering levers were applied, rotating the tank about its own axis. This gave a most useful turn facility in confined spaces.

A measure of skill was required of the driver to get the best out of Centurion, but the engine had a lot of torque and control was responsive. With a good driver a sustained cross-country speed of the order of 15mph was possible with minimal crew discomfort, ensuring that they arrived on the battlefield in a fit state to fight.

Fighting compartment

The power-operated turret contained the main armament and auxiliary weapons, with the wireless sets mounted in a recess at the

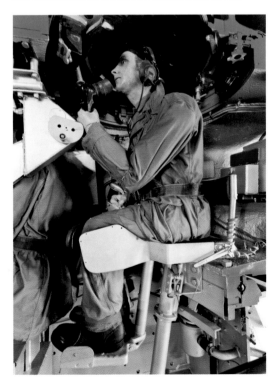

RIGHT The essence of a proficient tank crew is their close cooperation in their individual roles. Any tank is a means to provide direct fire on the battlefield in an armour protected vehicle manoeuvring across broken ground while supported by other arms. It is the role of the tank commander to acquire targets for the gunner to engage with the appropriate ammunition provided by the loader. The faster this process is undertaken is the key to survival on the battlefield since the tank that acquires and engages the enemy tank first is the one that lives to fight another day. On Centurion, the commander (right) observed the battlefield either from his open hatch or from under armour through the episcopes of his rotatable cupola.

rear. The commander was situated at the right-hand rear of the turret, with a vision cupola fitted in the roof plate over his position for all-round observation with full protection. Either of two types of cupola could be fitted. The early type No 2 Mark 1 had nine episcopes, eight No 7 Mark 1 and one No 8 Mark 1, while the later type No 2 Mark 2 had seven episcopes No 7 Mark 1, a commander's sight No 4 Mark 1, and one episcope No 8 Mark 1. Both types were fitted with ×10 periscopic binoculars. The cupola could be traversed by gear or by hand. It was fitted with a circular hatch, spring-assisted in operation, that could be secured in three open positions: vertical, oblique or horizontal.

Introduced in April 1954, the No 4 Mark 1 RCP (reflector-cum-periscope) sight was a significant advance in target acquisition. Previously, when the commander sighted a target he rotated the turret using his power traverse override control and aligned the main armament with the target by means of the blade vane sight mounted on the turret roof forward of the cupola. As this gave only an approximate line of sight, the gunner was often unable to see through his ×6 periscope inconspicuous targets that the commander had observed through his ×10 peri-binoculars. The RCP sight overcame this problem by means of a linkage between the gunner's and commander's sights, whereby both crewmen observed the same angle and field of view simultaneously. As the commander aligned the aiming point in his sight on the target, the gunner saw exactly the same in his, and had only to adjust for range before engagement. This markedly reduced the target-acquisition time that is fundamental to survival on the battlefield; the tank crew who are able to engage and hit a target the quickest are the crew that will survive.

The gunner was positioned to the right-hand side of the turret alongside the main armament, forward of the commander. Controls for using the armament were located convenient to his left and right hands, and the ×6 periscopic sight AFV Mark 1 or Mark 1/1 to his front, with the range gear and sight mounting No 1. The main armament of Centurion Mark 3 was the Ordnance 20-pounder Tank Mark 1 gun of 3.3in calibre. Four marks of 20-pounder barrels were used on Centurion Marks 1, 1/1, 1/2 and 1/3. Of these, Marks 1 and 1/2 Type A barrels had threads for the attachment of a muzzle brake, but this was not fitted and a counterweight was substituted to rebalance the gun. Marks 1/1 and 1/3 Type B barrels had, instead, a cylindrical fume extractor down the barrel but without the muzzle weight. The Type B barrel was introduced in December 1954 and was retrospectively fitted to most Centurions Mark 3.

The 20-pounder gun and coaxial Besa machine gun were supported and protected by a rectangular mantlet, which was usually fitted with a canvas cover to exclude dust and rain. The 20-pounder gun was a multi-purpose weapon designed to fire high-velocity armour-piercing shot and HE against unarmoured targets. It also fired canister shot, smoke shells and practice rounds. The fixed ammunition was hand-loaded into the side-opening breech and fired by electric primer. Recoil was absorbed by two buffer cylinders housed on each side of the gun cradle and attached to the gun mounting. Spent cases were ejected automatically backwards into a turret bin and disposed of through a port in the loader's side of the turret.

Perhaps the most significant advance in the Centurion was in the fire control system incorporating stabilisation of the gun mounting in azimuth and elevation that, for the first time, allowed accurate firing on the move. Gun controls in early Centurions Mark 3 were of the FVGCE No 1 Mark. 3/1 type, but after October 1950 the No 1 Mark 4 was installed. For indirect or semi-indirect shooting the gun was laid for line initially by the commander using the blade vane sight No. 9 on the turret roof, and subsequently by the gunner using the traverse indicator No 1 Mark 1 in the turret, and for elevation by means of the clinometer attached to the sight mechanism. For direct shooting from a stationary vehicle, the gunner laid the gun for line by either manual or electric turret traverse. He then applied the estimated range to the range drum and selected ammunition scale. As the gunner's sight was geared directly to the range drum, it pivoted at an angle proportionate to the drum setting. Movement of the gun in elevation also rotated the sight, and once a central point of aim had been taken on the target by means of the gunner's handwheel or elevation control, the gun was at the elevation appropriate to the range set and ready to fire.

For firing on the move, the Metrovick stabilisation system was brought into operation. As the tank moved across country its pitch and direction altered the gun in azimuth and elevation in relation to the original gun setting. These deviations were sensed by two restrained gyroscopes; appropriate corrections were transmitted via an amplifier to the metadyne generator, as elevation and traverse servo-motors returned the gun to its original heading.

The electro-mechanical Metrovick stabilisation system has been very successful in service and, although marginally more complex than hydraulic systems, it has proved to be more reliable and less vulnerable in battle. However, a popular misconception has arisen concerning the stabiliser, which is often thought to be a 'magic eye' that fixes the gun on the target irrespective of tank movement. This is not so. With the stabiliser engaged by means of the gunner's spade grip traversing handle, changes in azimuth were corrected and the gun stayed on its bearing relative to hull movement, but it was still necessary for the gunner to make fine corrections for loss of lay by inclining his spade grip to the appropriate extent. Similarly for elevation, as the tank pitched over undulating ground the stabiliser maintained the gun on its

LEFT For closer viewing of a potential target, the commander employed his x10 Peri-binoculars for accurate identification and the estimated range. He then informed the gunner (left) of these coordinates who initiated the engagement via his x6 periscopic sight. Once the target was acquired by the gunner, be it a tank or soft-skin vehicle, the commander ordered the loader to select the appropriate main armament round and the engagement began.

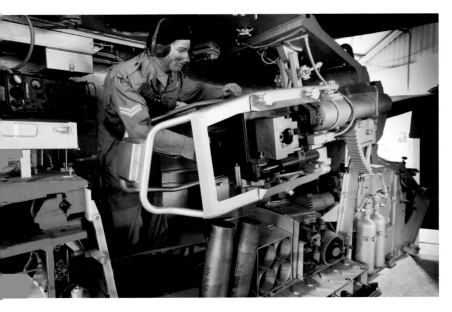

ABOVE The task of the loader/wireless operator was highly important within Centurion and arguably the most arduous since he had two distinct roles to undertake. Firstly he maintained communications with other tanks and units by using the Wireless Sets No 19 and No 38. As the loader, he was responsible for keeping the ammunition in good condition to minimize the chances of misfires. He also needed to know where each and every different type of ammunition were stowed so that he could respond to the commander's fire orders with the appropriate round as quickly as possible. The loader was also responsible for serving and loading the coaxial machine gun as well as helping the gunner to maintain the main armament.

original bearing, but the gunner had to apply manual corrections on his elevation controller. Once the gunner had acquired the ability to work in co-ordination with the stabiliser, and not to anticipate its corrections as he saw his point of aim deviating in his sight, the system was very effective, but at all times it required the gunner's skill to maintain the gun on the target.

Although it was possible to fire AP rounds on the move, it was preferable to halt to obtain optimum results. In these circumstances the stabiliser was a great asset, since while moving the gunner held the gun in the target area and as the tank halted it required only a split second or so to lay the true point of aim and engage the target. Firing HE on the move under stabilised control was very effective, as was speculative 'prophylactic' coaxial machine gun fire against hedgerows and ditches that might conceal enemy infantry.

The third crew member in the turret, the loader/operator, worked on the left-hand side of the main armament. Besides being responsible for loading the main armament, and loading and clearing stoppages on the coaxial Besa machine gun, he tuned and serviced the wireless installation. Centurions up to and including early Mark 3s, were fitted with the No 19 WT and No 38 AFV sets. Many of these were of Second World War vintage and in dubious condition; they might also have been made for overseas armies, causing considerable confusion if the instructions were

found to be in Cyrillic or Chinese characters. The WS 19 Mark 3 was divided into A and B sets and intercom; the A set was for tank communication within the squadron, while the B set was for communications within the troop. Orders from the commander were relayed to crew members through the vehicle's intercom (IC) system. An infantry telephone was fitted to the rear hull plate of the vehicle and connected to the vehicle IC. Command and control tanks had a second No 19 set for communication with higher formations. Three 4ft sections of aerial were provided for the A set but only one section was normally erected in order to avoid entanglement with trees and overhead wires; this gave a range of 5 miles, depending on terrain and conditions, which was sufficient for most purposes. The No 38 set, replaced in 1950 by the No 88 Type AFV, was used for co-operation with infantry. These wireless sets were superseded in 1956 by VHF equipment. A typical later Centurion had one SR C42 VHF transceiver for armour command links incorporating the crew IC, and one SR B47 VHF transceiver for use on infantry nets.

The secondary armament of Centurion Mark 3 was the 7.92mm Besa Mark 3/1 machine gun mounted coaxially with the main armament in the mantlet, and the same gun controls were used for elevating or depressing the machine gun. Although an effective weapon, the Besa was never really satisfactory in Centurion as it was prone to frequent stoppages and gave off toxic fumes, much to the discomfort of the crew. Many veteran 'tankies' had served through the war in American tanks mounting the reliable 0.30in (.30cal) M1919 Browning machine gun, and they never came to terms with the Besa in the post-war years (in 1955 it was replaced by the Browning). The machine gun fired four types of ammunition at a rate of fire of 450–550 rounds per minute, for engaging unarmoured targets and personnel at short and medium ranges. The maximum effective range for direct shooting from a stationary vehicle was 1,600yd and, when moving, up to 800yd; semi-indirect fire was possible up to 2,000yd. The four types of ammunition were AP, ball, tracer and incendiary, and were fired in the sequence tracer/AP/ball/AP/tracer/AP/ball/incendiary, known by the phonetic acronym TABA-TABI.

The Centurion Mark 3 carried 65 rounds of 20-pounder ammunition of which 10 were readily accessible to the loader. Some 16 boxes of 225-round belts of 7.92mm Besa ammunition were carried, making a total of 3,600 rounds. All main armament rounds were stowed below the level of the turret ring, as follows:

20-pounder
- 4 rounds in ready bin
- 4 rounds in sliding racks
- 16 rounds in four bins under floor, left-hand side of fighting compartment
- 20 rounds in bin left of driver's compartment
- 14 rounds in four bins under floor, on right side of fighting compartment
- 5 rounds in bin under floor to rear of rotary base junction
- 2 rounds in bin on right side of rear bulkhead.

7.92mm Besa
- 6 boxes, front left-hand turret wall
- 2 boxes in bin left of 20-round bin
- 6 boxes in two bins on front right side of fighting compartment near driver
- 2 boxes in bin on right wall near rear bulkhead.

A six-barrel smoke-grenade discharger No 1 Mark 1 was fitted externally on each side of the turret forward of the stowage bins, firing No 80 White Phosphorus grenades to provide an immediate smokescreen at short range for self-protection. Each discharger had two sets of three barrels mounted in order to spread the grenades out laterally to a range of approximately 60yd; the dischargers were operated electrically from inside the turret, but once fired had to be reloaded outside the vehicle. The loader also operated the 2in bomb thrower Mark 2, located in the turret roof beside the loader's periscope in a rotatable plate which was meant to traverse the bomb thrower when not in use so that the breech was clear of the loader's head. The bomb thrower was aligned approximately fore-and-aft for loading and firing, and laid for line by traversing the turret. It was a breech-loading weapon with a simple falling-block type breech mechanism, to provide smokescreens at variable ranges out to 300yd. It was provided with two types of smoke ammunition: the Mark 1 with instantaneous action and the Mark 3 (White Phosphorus), which burst on impact. Other rounds were available such as HE and illuminating flare. (The latter was much prized by tank crews: they dismantled the flares and used the silk parachutes for handkerchiefs.) The bomb thrower was never popular as it intruded into the turret space; a muffled curse from the loader was a sure sign that he had once again hit his head on the breech. With the multi-barrel smoke dischargers on the turret, the bomb thrower was in any case somewhat redundant and it was rarely used in battle, although crews occasionally bombarded opposing tanks or umpires with smoke bombs during field exercises. It was discontinued on late-production Mark 3s and subsequently removed from earlier vehicles.

Other crew weapons carried inside the tank included one 9mm Sten sub-machine gun with 16 magazines; 9 mixed grenades No 36 (fragmentation), No 80 (smoke) and No 83 (coloured smoke); and a signal pistol with 12 cartridges.

Engine compartment

The engine compartment was separated from the fighting compartment by a fireproof bulkhead incorporating the turret ventilation system, charging set, engine controls, and a two-round ammunition bin.

BELOW Centurion Mark 3 engine compartment.

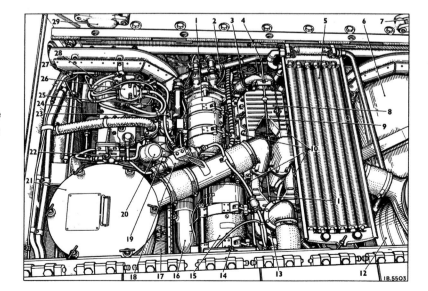

Removal of the ammunition bin and bulkhead 'kidney' plate allowed access to certain engine assemblies such as magnetos, starter motor and coolant pump.

The tank was powered by a Meteor Mark 4B or 4B/1 12-cylinder V-type liquid-cooled overhead-valve petrol engine developing 650bhp at 2,250rpm. The choice of a petrol engine for Centurion was determined by the wartime policy of obtaining the widest possible amount of fuels from a given quantity of crude oil; the Royal Navy had priority for diesel oil, the RAF for high-octane aviation fuel, with the Army dependent on petroleum spirit. The use of petrol for tanks was therefore a deliberate decision, reiterated in 1951, for the economic division of available supplies of crude oil – but a petrol engine has a lower thermal efficiency than a diesel engine, and therefore a higher fuel consumption. The major shortcoming of the Meteor engine was its petrol consumption of approximately 3–4 gallons to the mile across country, and an inadequate range of 32 miles before refuelling was necessary.

The Meteor had two banks of six cylinders arranged in a 60-degree Vee, and was lubricated by a sump force-feed system incorporating a pressure and a double-scavenge pump. The engine's 33-gallon pressurised liquid cooling system was sealed to a pressure of 10lb/psi, thus raising the boiling point of the coolant – an anti-freeze mixture of ethylene glycol and water – to a temperature of 239°F. The fuel system was provided with two tanks, one on each side of the engine; the right-hand tank had a capacity of 59 gallons and the left-hand one of 62 gallons. The fuel used was petrol of not less than 80 octane, delivered to the carburettor by two mechanically operated diaphragm pumps located on the front of the engine. The two twin-choke updraft Zenith carburettors were situated between the cylinder banks at the front and rear.

Respiratory air was drawn through the engine deck louvres by the suction side of the engine fans and, after passing through two oil-bath type air cleaners mounted in the rear corners of the engine compartment, into an air trunk located between the carburettor to the coolant-jacketed induction manifold. Ignition was provided by two magnetos, each

embodying an automatic advance and retard coupling, and to facilitate starting a booster coil enhancing the intensity of spark was fitted. Spring-loaded governors in the rotors limited the engine revs to 2,250rpm by shorting the high-tension (HT) leads at that speed. This action resulted in unburnt mixture passing to the exhausts and exploding there; consequently, driving 'on the governors' was bad practice from an operational point of view.

Two sparking plugs were fitted in each cylinder, one on the inlet side, the other on the exhaust side. The vehicle was provided with a 24V nominal electrical system. Current was supplied by four 6V batteries connected in series and located beneath the fighting compartment floor. The batteries were charged either by a generator fitted to the top of the main engine or by a generator driven from an auxiliary four-cylinder side-valve Morris USHNM Mark 2 or 2/1 petrol engine located in the front left-hand corner of the engine compartment. It was independent of the main engine except for the cooling and fuel systems, and could be run whether the main engine was in use or not. The set was run when the power traverse, radios or the essential Vessel Boiling Electric, known as the BV, were in use or when the batteries were in a low state of charge.

A Ki-Gass priming system provided the means of injecting a spray of fuel into the induction manifold for starting the engine in very cold weather. The engine cooling fans were mounted between the engine and transmission compartments. Non-respiratory air passed over the engine, up through two swivelling radiators mounted near-horizontally over the gearbox and out of the vehicle through the rear outlet louvres.

Transmission compartment

Power from the main engine was transmitted through a Borg & Beck triple dry clutch to the transversely mounted Merritt-Brown Z51R gearbox. The transmission consisted of a combined change speed and steering mechanism. Steering of the vehicle was achieved by means of brakes situated on either side of the gearbox and mechanically operated by the two steering levers in the driver's compartment. The drive from the output epicyclic gears at each side of the gearbox was transmitted through an internally toothed coupling ring and an externally toothed driving shaft to the final drives. This system of steering reduced the loss of power from the engine to the tracks and provided a positive turning circle in each gear, the radius of the circle being 16ft in bottom gear and 140ft in top gear.

Two final drive and sprocket assemblies were mounted at the rear of the vehicle. Each final drive assembly comprised a double reduction train of spur gears, whereby the speed of output from the gearbox was reduced to the ratio of 7.47:1 and the torque effort to the tracks was increased.

Gear engaged	Gear ratio	Max speed	Turning circle
5	1.341:1	21.5	140ft
4	1.807:1	15.0	104ft
3	2.854:1	10.1	66ft
2	4.593:1	6.3	41ft
1	11.641:1	2.5	16ft
Low Reverse	22.910:1	1.26	skid
High Reverse	3.859:1	7.4	49ft

Suspension and tracks

The vehicle was supported on six suspension units, three on each side. Each unit incorporated three horizontal springs mounted concentrically and guided by a central rod and tube. The two outer springs were of equal length, the inner spring was shorter and only effective after initial deflection of the roadwheel had occurred. The assembly was mounted between knife-edges carried on the axle arms. The front and rear suspension units incorporated four hydraulic shock absorbers mounted inboard of the assembly bracket. Each shock absorber was connected to the axle arm by a lever and link.

Each unit was fitted with two pairs of rubber-tyred roadwheels. All roadwheels were interchangeable to any position. The top of each track was supported on four double rubber-tyred and two single all-steel guide rollers. The double rollers supported the top rim of each track and the single rollers, secured at the front and rear,

prevented the track fouling the front suspension unit and final drive housing respectively.

The track was of cast manganese steel construction, and a new track comprised 108 links. Each link was 24in wide at 5.5in pitch, and had a spud to engage the ground and a horn on the inner face to guide the track on the wheels. Track adjustment was achieved by movement of the front idler wheel on an eccentric axle mounted at the front of the vehicle. As the track stretched in use, the idler wheel was moved forward to maintain the correct tension. When no further movement forward was allowable, gauged by the number of threads exposed, the track was broken and a link removed. The track was normally replaced after the removal of seven links. Six detachable skirting plates – known as bazooka plates – with three on each side provided additional protection for the hull sides and suspension.

ABOVE Centurion Mark 3 transmission compartment.

BELOW The Centurion incorporated a Horstmann-type suspension with the four-wheel bogie units attached to the exterior of the hull that were simpler to replace after mine damage and allowed for the increasing weight of later marks of the tank.

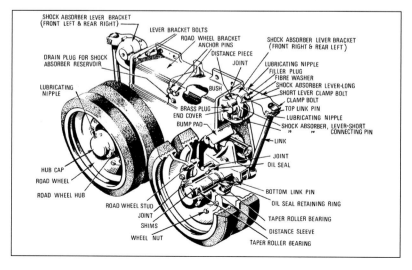

Chapter Three

Operating the Centurion

A first parade is carried out at the beginning of each day. It ensures all the essential systems on the tank are in full working order and that fluid levels are sufficient. It also highlights any defects and gives the crew a chance to repair them in a safe environment. This chapter describes a first parade as carried out by Tank Museum staff.

OPPOSITE 44BA17 was one of the last Centurion gun tanks to see service with the British Army in the guise of the Centurion 105 AVRE as used by the Armoured Engineers. It is now the main Centurion runner at the Tank Museum, Bovington. It has been named CHATTY after one of the most ebullient characters that worked at the museum driving and maintaining the tanks in the collection. In essence the contents of the Centurion Owner's Workshop Manual remains inside the heads of people like Chatty and his colleagues.

The Centurion featured in this chapter is a Mark 12 Armoured Vehicle Royal Engineers. There are some minor differences in layout between the AVRE and the standard 'gun' tank. The first parade procedures in this chapter relate to this vehicle.

First parade

Main engine oil check

The engine is lubricated by a dry sump force-feed lubrication system that holds 14 gallons of OMD-110 oil. The filler is located in the transmission compartment.

The five transmission compartment covers are numbered from right to left, and must be opened in order. They hinge forwards and, with the turret at 12 o'clock, they rest against the stowage bin.

- Lift No 1 transmission compartment cover [1]. Commander to assist Driver.
- Locate and remove engine oil filler cap by hand [2].
- Fully remove dipstick [3].
- The dipstick is marked 'HIGH' and 'LOW'. Ensure oil level is between these two marks.
- Top up as needed, replace dipstick and filler cap.
- Once the engine is running and warmed up, the oil should reach the 'HIGH' mark.

Main engine coolant check

The main engine coolant is an anti-freeze mixture of ethylene glycol and water. The system has a capacity of 33 gallons, and is pressurised at 10lb/psi to prevent it boiling under normal operating conditions. Ensure the engine is cold, otherwise the system will still be pressurised.

Open transmission compartment covers No 1, No 2 and No 3. Commander to assist Driver. (The photographs also show the radiator raised. This is not required to carry out this check.)

- Locate coolant filler cap [1].
- Loosen with spanner, then open by hand [2].
- Check level, top up to the top of the filler tube if necessary.

Check main fuel level

Early Centurions have two petrol tanks, one on each side of the engine. The Mark 7 and later variants have an additional third tank at the rear. The capacity of the tanks varies depending on the version; on the two-tank Mark 3 the right tank holds 59 gallons and the left 62. On the three-tank Mark 8 this becomes 56 and 77 gallons respectively, with a 95-gallon rear tank. Each tank must be filled separately. The filler caps are protected by armoured covers. They are connected to the tanks with tube and hose connections that need periodic inspection to ensure they are intact and that petrol has not leaked into the engine compartment, posing a serious fire risk.

The left- and right-hand tanks are connected to fuel gauges in the driver's compartment. Filling is therefore a two-man job, with one man filling the tank and the other closely watching the gauges. The rear tank fuel gauge is mounted on the tank itself and the driver has no way of checking its level from his seat. The fuel tap controls which tank the petrol is drawn from. It has either three or four positions: 'OFF', 'LEFT', 'RIGHT' and (on three-tank vehicles) 'REAR'. It is located at the left rear of the fighting compartment and operated by the loader.

Gearbox oil check

The oil in the gearbox is delivered under pressure to the bearings using a pump. The system holds 4.5 gallons of OC-600 oil.

- Open all five transmission compartment covers. Commander to assist Driver.
- Lift both radiators to vertical. They will rest securely [1] [2].
- Locate the gearbox oil dipstick [3] [4].
- Unscrew and remove dipstick by hand and check oil level. It should reach the 'HIGH' mark on the dipstick [5].
- To top up locate and open filler cap. Top up to 'HIGH' mark.
- Close transmission compartment covers.

(These photographs only show the crew checking the gearbox oil level. This can be done with just the right-hand radiator raised. The filler for topping up is located under the left-hand radiator.)

Charging set oil check

The charging set is a small engine used to charge the vehicle batteries, to operate the BV, the radio sets or the main gun equipment at any time when the main engine is not running, or to supplement the main engine generator.

It uses the same coolant and fuel systems as the main engine, but is otherwise independent. Its oil supply requires 7 pints of OMD-110. It is located in the engine compartment.

The five engine compartment covers are interlocking. Numbering from the right, it is necessary to open No 1 and No 3 before No 2, and No 3 and No 5 before No 4. They open backwards, resting on the transmission compartment covers.

- Each engine compartment cover must be lifted through the gap between the two turret stowage bins [1]. This means the turret must be traversed slightly to raise each cover.
- The Commander assists the Driver with lifting the covers. The Gunner traverses the turret as ordered.
- Lift engine compartment covers No 3, No 4 and No 5. (In these photographs No 5 has been lowered again.)
- Locate charging set dipstick [2].
- Remove dipstick and check oil level [3]. To top up, locate and remove filler cap. Top up as required [4].
- Close engine compartment covers.

Starting the charging set

On early models of Centurion the charging set controls are located on the left side of the rear bulkhead and operated by the Loader under instruction from the Driver. On later variants, including this AVRE, they have been moved to the right-hand side of the Driver's compartment.

- Rotate starter carburettor control (the lever closest to the hull wall) anti-clockwise to the first stop. Only use the second stop in severely cold weather.
- Rotate throttle control (the lever closest to the driver) fully clockwise to the closed position. Turn on ignition switch and check that warning lights illuminate.
- Press starter switch. When set starts, allow it to warm up for a few minutes.

Slowly rotate starter carburettor control lever clockwise to the closed position.
- Slowly rotate throttle lever anti-clockwise to the open position. Check the ammeter is showing a charge.

Starting the main engine
- Set fuel tap to 'LEFT'.
- Ensure parking brake is on, both steering levers are forward and the gear lever is in neutral.
- Close hand throttle by pulling it fully out.

- Switch on ignition switch and depress clutch pedal.
- Press starter button. Engine should start. If it does not, release the button, pull strangler lever fully back to 'ON' position, and press starter button again.
- As soon as the engine starts, release starter button. If the strangler lever was pulled back, push it fully forwards.
- Check oil pressure is rising, increase engine speed to 1,500rpm using hand throttle and release clutch pedal.

For a first parade, run the engine for around 5 minutes then switch off and recheck oil level. For driving, set engine speed to 1,000–1,200rpm using hand throttle. Allow engine temperature to rise to approximately 130°F before attempting to move off. This should take around 10 minutes.

Under normal conditions, move off in 2nd gear. Only use 1st on a difficult gradient or in confined spaces.

Track inspection

Inspecting the track requires three crewmen. The Driver moves the tank and the other two crew inspect one track each. They are looking for damage, cracks and faulty or loose track pins and circlips.

To inspect the inside of the track, the crewmen stand back to back in front of the vehicle. The Driver slowly reverses the tank to allow them to see each link in turn.

To inspect the outside, they stand one on each side of the tank facing inwards, while the Driver drives slowly forwards. [1]

When new, a Centurion track has 108 links. The track stretches in use, which increases the amount of slack present. As a track slackens, it is more likely to break or be thrown loose, immobilising the vehicle and needing a lot of hard work to repair. Checking the track tension is therefore a daily task for the crew.

- With the vehicle on hard, level ground, remove the centre side skirt.
- Use a neutral turn (turning the vehicle on the spot) to gather all the slack along the top side of the track. Turn in the opposite direction to the track being checked, *ie* turn left to check the right-hand track.
- Check between the second and third return rollers. There should be 1–1.5in (25–38mm) of sag in the track at this point. Officially this should be done with a length of string or a straight edge, but experienced crews could do it by eye [2].
- Repeat neutral turn and check on the other track. If the tension is correct, replace the side skirts. If not, the track must be tensioned (see below).

Conclude first parade by shutting down charging set and main engine, and closing any open engine or transmission compartment covers.

As well as assisting the Driver where noted, the Commander, Loader and Gunner have their own checks and tests to carry out during a first parade.

Other checks and inspections

Drive sprocket tooth inspection

The drive sprocket is the only powered wheel on a tank. On Centurions it is the rearmost wheel. The teeth will wear out, and have to be inspected every 250 miles. This is a task for a REME vehicle mechanic rather than the crew.

The sprocket teeth wear most at the darkened areas on the photograph [1 and 2]. A gauge is used to measure this wear. The sprockets are to be replaced after wear reaches between 0.100 and 0.125in (2.54–3.18mm)

Track tensioning

This is done by moving the idler wheel at the front of the tank.

- Locate and slacken pinch bolt on idler wheel adjuster nut. This is located at the very front of the tank, behind the idler wheel [3]. (Later Centurions use a removable locking plate instead of a pinch bolt.)
- Carry out neutral turn as per the instructions for track inspection (see p. 78) to gather slack on top of track.
- Using track adjusting tool and extension [4], tighten adjuster nut until track is correctly tensioned [5]. This may require the full weight of two crewmen.
- Tighten pinch bolt or replace locking plate.
- Replace side skirt.
- If the adjuster nut cannot be tightened further, then a track link must be removed. This can be done a maximum of seven times before the whole track must be replaced.

DRIVING THE CENTURION

Keith Glenn, Tank Museum Workshop Technician and ex-4th Royal Tank Regiment

I was introduced to the Centurion tank in Berlin at the age of 18. This huge green machine was to be entrusted to me – what an awesome thought!

Like any older car the basic controls are easy to master and can be learned in a few minutes. However, to be able to give a safe and comfortable ride to one's crew requires practice; the acquisition of these skills and techniques takes time. Above all the watchword is 'anticipation', which means looking at the ground conditions, any potential obstacles or tight turns. Whenever tanks moved in Berlin there was usually a police escort to clear the roads but, on occasion, we were unescorted and this meant negotiating the traffic on sometimes icy cobbled streets.

The Centurion has no additional assistance to the mechanical operation of the steering, brakes or clutch and requires some physical effort. This means the driver can become tired and other members of the crew are needed to give the driver rest spells. Many gear changes are needed to get the best out of a Centurion and double-declutching is the norm. Keeping the tank moving is probably the most difficult task as it can slow down quickly. No trouble when changing down but experienced drivers soon learned the 'stick change', which keeps momentum on the up changes.

Some of the early lessons learned included the fact that the main and steering brakes fade rapidly with repeated application and the driver has to make allowances for this. Crossing any obstacle or undertaking a tight turn means being in the right gear at the right time to keep the tank moving. Going over a knife-edge has the saying 'up in 1, down in 5'.

Fortunately the Centurion has a fairly high clearance above the driver's head so approach marches can be done with the hatches open. When closed down, visibility is restricted but the periscopes pivot to left and right and are mounted fairly high, giving the driver a reasonable field of view. This is not as bad as some other tanks but the driver still needs to have total confidence in the other members of the crew.

The Centurion, compared to more modern tanks, has plenty of room internally and externally for personal kit. So life can be more comfortable. Having a boiling vessel helped with creature comforts and was the envy of any supporting infantry. A quicker method of heating food was to put tins of 'compo' on the exhaust manifolds. The only method of heating was the duct in the turret from the auxiliary generator, so the driver was always cold in Germany.

Now, some 50-plus years on, I am lucky enough to be able to drive the Tank Museum's various Centurion-based vehicles such as the AVRE, ARV and BARV. Due to the passage of time they seem taller, larger and with more sharp projections than I recall. However, after a few nervous laps of the arena I feel privileged to feel the unique experience of the Centurion again.

Bombing up

Loading ammunition, or 'bombing up' was a job for at least two men, and ideally more.

Starting with the Mark 7, a loading port was added to the left of the hull, which was connected to a hole in the side skirt by a removable chute [1] [2]. As all ammunition was stowed in the hull, this made loading easier as it had previously required either using the roof hatches or the turret port [3]. However it entered the tank, each round then had to be stowed individually by the single crewman inside. The ammunition was stored in a number of racks and bins around the hull and under the floor. There was no single turret position

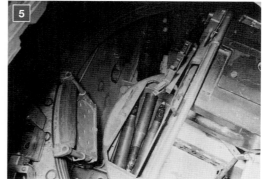

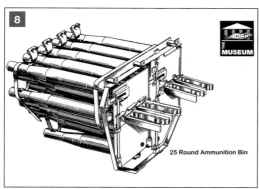

25 Round Ammunition Bin

that allowed access to all of them at once, so it had to be traversed several times during loading [4–8].

Between 63 and 73 rounds could be carried. This number varied depending on the size of the gun and on the arrangement of the ammunition stowage on different marks of Centurion [9] [10].

The largest ammunition used, 105mm, weighed between 18 and 21kg (39–46lb) and was 850–950mm (33–37in) long. Bombing up was therefore a slow and laborious process that involved a lot of heavy lifting and awkward movement in a very confined space.

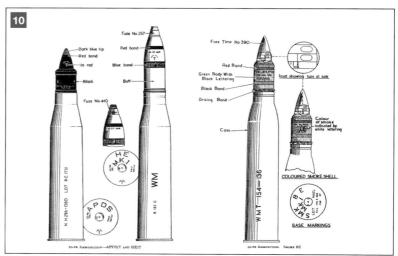

Chapter Four

Specialist Centurion variants

Having devised the 'Funnies' of 79th Armoured Division to breach the German defences on D-Day, the concept was continued post-war with a range of specialised AFVs developed on the Centurion chassis. Their fundamental purpose was to enhance the mobility of armoured formations on the battlefield both in attack or defence.

OPPOSITE The Centurion ARV Mark 2 had a crew of four REME technicians qualified in different trades that included a recovery mechanic, vehicle mechanic, gun fitter or electrician, so that all the aspects of a defective AFV could be addressed in the field. The ARV Mark 2 was capable of a direct pull of 30 tons and by means of 3:1 tackle, as here, up to 90 tons – more than sufficient for all but the most bogged tanks.

The ill-fated Dieppe Raid of August 1942 had emphasised the need for specialised combat support AFVs to lead the assault against *Festung Europa,* and consequently a wide range of ingenious (if sometimes bizarre) devices was developed, based on the chassis of existing tanks. Those that proved effective were incorporated into the largest British armoured formation of the Second World War – the 79th Armoured Division, commanded by Major General Sir Percy Hobart. Colloquially known as 'The Funnies', they played an invaluable part in the all-arms battle, from the D-Day landings of June 1944 throughout the whole campaign in north-west Europe.

After the war it was proposed to develop a range of vehicles of a similar specialist nature, including two designs of AVRE (Armoured Vehicle Royal Engineers), a flail mine destroyer, an ARV (armoured recovery vehicle), an APC (armoured personnel carrier), an ARK (armoured ramp carrier), and various SPGs (self-propelled guns) and support vehicles for the Royal Artillery. As the A41 was considered incapable of being adapted to this multitude of roles without extensive redesign, it was decided to develop the A45 to become the FV201. This universal tank would form the basis of these specialised vehicles, with the attendant advantages of standardisation on a single chassis. However, as already described, the

FV200 series never came to fruition except as the Conqueror Heavy Gun Tank, and the only variant to enter service was the FV219 ARV. The plethora of designs absorbed a considerable amount of research and development effort and delayed the introduction of specialised vehicles based on the Centurion chassis – which, despite the fears of the General Staff, proved extremely versatile and capable of being converted to most of the desired roles.

The first armoured recovery vehicles

The Second World War had demonstrated the fundamental importance of efficient repair and recovery facilities. During the fighting in North Africa the majority of the many tanks that suffered battle damage sustained only minor damage, principally to suspensions and tracks from mines and to turrets from gunfire. Approximately half of those disabled by gunfire and almost all by mines were capable of repair. However, it was mechanical failure (whether due to bad driving, poor maintenance, unfavourable terrain or just ordinary wear and tear) that absorbed the greater proportion of recovery resources, and the need for an ARV capable of recovering casualties in the forward battle area proved to be of the utmost importance.

When the Centurion entered service the only support vehicles available were the existing wartime designs, and it soon became apparent that these were inadequate for the recovery of the heavier Centurion. At the time the regimental LAD (Light Aid Detachment) and REME personnel were equipped with the Diamond T tractor, Scammell 6×4 recovery vehicle and Churchill ARV. The first two vehicles had poor cross-country performance and limited winching capacity, and were unable to tow a disabled Centurion. The Churchill ARV Mark 2 was capable of winching and towing a Centurion, but with a top speed of only 14mph it was unable to keep up with Centurion formations and was prone to breakdowns. The only alternative was to use a Centurion gun tank to tow the casualty, and although this was frequently done it naturally met with stiff opposition from regimental commanders and General Staff officers.

BELOW One of the very first Centurions to be converted to the recovery role was Centurion Mark 3 01ZR91 of the 8th King's Royal Irish Hussars (8KRIH) in Korea. It is seen here in its Centurion Tug configuration with its REME crew as they await a call to come to the rescue of the Centurions and vehicles of 5th Royal Tank Regiment.

Events in Korea likewise demonstrated the need for a purpose-built recovery vehicle for Centurion. As an interim measure a battle-damaged gun tank was converted at Kure in Japan to become a towing vehicle by the removal of the turret and ammunition stowage bins, while other hulls came from Germany. Known as Centurion Tugs, they were issued on a scale of one per squadron with one in regimental HQ. They served primarily as supply vehicles, carrying ammunition and stores to the exposed hilltop positions where the gun tanks acted in their fire support role. These positions were often inaccessible to wheeled vehicles, and as the supply routes were subjected to persistent mortar and artillery fire, the armoured Centurion Tugs proved invaluable for this task. As a secondary role they were employed as towing vehicles to recover battle casualties, but, lacking winching equipment, they were unable to extricate bogged vehicles.

Pending the development of a purpose-built ARV, similar conversions were undertaken at the 27th REME Command Workshops at Warminster, Wiltshire, and at the 7th Armoured Division REME Workshops in Germany. The first Centurion 'Tower' entered service with BAOR in 1952. The conversion was carried out on Centurion Mark 1, 2 and 3 hulls. The turret and all fire control equipment were removed but the turret ring and traverse gear were retained. A capstan drum fitted to the turret ring could still be rotated by either hand or power traverse. The purpose of this drum was to provide stowage for a 300ft, 20-ton SWL steel wire rope; it must be stressed that this capstan drum was purely a means of stowing the wire rope and was not, as often thought, a winch. A fixed, non-rotating steel plate was fitted above the capstan drum. This top plate had twin sliding hatches to allow entry to the internal crew space and stowage lockers. Twin windscreens and two large stowage bins were located above it. A hinged 'wishbone' towing link and a fixed strongpoint anchor were attached to the rear of the hull. A fairlead guide roller was fitted to the top of the left-hand trackguard to prevent snagging of the rope when removing or replacing it after use. The front of the hull was fitted with a 'pushing post' at the centre, attachment points for the stowage of two

30-ton SWL 'D'-shackles, two ground anchor bars (a further six of these and ten spikes were stowed in the cover bins) and four hardwood blocks. On top of the rear hull, a loose 100ft, 30-ton SWL steel wire rope was carried, and stowage brackets on the rear trackguards held four gun planks, an 'A'-frame tow bar and spare track links. An auxiliary 250-gallon fuel tank was fitted in place of the forward ammunition

ABOVE AND BELOW In the early days of Centurion service, the existing Armoured Recovery Vehicle (ARV), the Churchill ARV Mark 2, proved inadequate for the task due to its lack of speed and towing capacity together with the heavier weight of Centurion. As an interim measure pending the introduction of a purpose-designed Centurion ARV, various Centurion hulls were converted as Towers (as in towing and not a high building). *(Photograph REME Museum of Military Technology)*

BELOW With the turret removed, the Centurion Tower was considerably lighter than a gun tank and with the usual tweaking of the engine by REME fitters it was also faster, particularly on roads. Furthermore, it tended to skid on cornering and more so on cobblestones, as here, with the vehicle negotiating a sharp bend. Most Centurion Towers were subsequently converted to become proper ARVs, either Mark 1 or 2. *(Photograph REME Museum of Military Technology)*

stowage bin alongside the driver. The vehicle also carried oxyacetylene cutting and welding equipment, Nobel 808 plastic explosive for track cutting and special tools for engine and transmission repairs. It was equipped with a No 19 radio set and carried a crew of three: driver, commander and radio operator/fitter. The weight of the vehicle was approximately 43 tons with a rated top speed of 25mph, but the customary REME tuning of carburettors and isolation of ignition governors produced speeds of 30mph, as well as providing a welcome power bonus for uphill tows.

This Centurion Tower performed well in its role of removing casualties from the battlefield while providing armoured protection to REME personnel, but its greatest limitation remained the lack of winching equipment. To 'unditch' a casualty, the tug relied on its own tractive power and the assistance of steel wire ropes and snatch blocks. It could not itself recover a heavily bogged casualty, and in such cases had to call for assistance from Royal Engineer Caterpillar D8 crawler tractors with winches, or else work in conjunction with a number of

Scammells. It did, however, prove that there was a valid requirement for REME recovery teams in the forward battle area, and it laid the foundations for the introduction of the Centurion ARV Mark 1. After their replacement by the later types of ARV, the Centurion Tugs were employed on gunnery ranges as ammunition carriers and for towing range hulks. In January 1957, one Tower was used as the basis for the prototype Centurion BARV (Beach Armoured Recovery Vehicle).

The design of a purpose-built ARV began at FVRDE in 1951, but pending its introduction pressing demands from Korea and BAOR for a vehicle with a winching capability led to the development of the Centurion ARV Mark 1. This stop-gap was designed and produced in a remarkably short time by 13th REME Command Workshops in Aldershot based on Mark 1 and 2 hulls. The turret was replaced by a slab-sided armoured superstructure housing a 72bhp Bedford QL six-cylinder petrol engine driving an 18-ton SWL winch. The vehicle was fitted with a spade at the rear in order to anchor itself during winching operations, but this often proved

The Centurion ARV Mark 1 (Aldershot Pattern) was a stop-gap measure to address the deficiencies of the Churchill ARV Mark 2, although both vehicles shared the same winching equipment. Aldershot Pattern referred to where the conversions were undertaken at 13th REME Command Workshops. The Centurion ARV Mark 1 was based on Mark 1 and Mark 2 long hulls, hence the ribs on the transmission covers. The vehicle carried comprehensive recovery equipment but the rear spade proved to be too weak and tended to distort during heavy recovery operations, so it was often reinforced with strengthening ribs to prevent distortion.

RIGHT Physician heal thyself – a Centurion ARV Mark 1 of 5 RTR recovers a companion vehicle that has lost its track and sprocket wheel. The first Centurion ARV Mark 1s were completed in late 1951 and several were immediately despatched to Korea where they arrived in January 1952 to serve with the 5th Royal Inniskilling Dragoon Guards. One was issued to each sabre squadron with further ARVs with regimental headquarters and the REME Heavy Aid Detachment. Although a great improvement on the Churchill ARV, the vehicle lacked proper vision blocks for the commander and the top-mounted hatches made it hazardous to dismount when under mortar fire, unlike the Churchill ARV with its side doors between the tracks. Of particular note, the ARV in the background has been fitted with the commander's cupola of a Centurion gun tank to overcome the problem of lack of vision when under armour.

inadequate for the task. Despite frequent reinforcement by welding steel plates to it, the spade was prone to distortion and cracking. The winch served to raise and lower the spade.

Stowage of ancillary recovery equipment was similar to that on the Centurion Tower, and included snatch blocks, 'A'-frame tow bar and towing hawsers. Gun planks, hardwood blocks, stowage bins, tool kits and jerrycans were attached to the superstructure. By means of the snatch blocks, a line-pull of 54 tons could be achieved. Access to the crew compartment was via two rear hatches in the turret roof, while two others forward of these gave access to the winch and winch engine.

Production began in 1951 at Aldershot, which provided the vehicle's designation: Centurion ARV Mark 1 (Aldershot Pattern). The first models completed were rushed to Korea, arriving in January 1952 to equip the HAD (Heavy Aid Detachment) REME of the 5th Royal Inniskilling Dragoon Guards. They proved to be a considerable improvement over previous recovery vehicles, but the access hatches in the turret roof were disliked. This was because, while entering or leaving the vehicle in forward areas, the crews were often exposed to sniper and mortar fire. Approximately 180 vehicles were built before

production ceased in 1957. Besides Korea, the Centurion ARV Mark 1 saw operational service with the British Army at Suez in 1956 and elsewhere in the Middle East. It was withdrawn from front-line service in 1959 but remained as a training vehicle well into the 1960s.

Centurion ARV Mark 2 (FV4006)

The design of a purpose-built recovery vehicle based on the Centurion began in 1951 at FVRDE. The basis of the ARV Mark 2 was a Mark 1, 2, 3 or 5 hull with an armoured superstructure in place of the turret, housing a winch powered by an auxiliary engine. The latter was either a Rolls-Royce B80 No 1 Mark 2P or B80 No 1 Mark 5P mounted in the winch compartment, driving an electric generator which supplied current to a motor below the winch and drove it by means of a roller chain. The winch was capable of producing a direct pull of 30 tons, or 90 tons when using 3:1 tackle, for which purpose pulley blocks were carried on the glacis plate. It was provided with 450ft of 1⅛-in diameter SWR cable, known universally as 'rope', with a useable length of 400ft.

A spade-type group anchor was fitted at the rear of the hull to prevent the ARV being dragged during heavy winch pulls; such pulls were, of course, made directly to the rear of the vehicle. An eye was welded on each side plate at the rear to form an anchorage for use when making side hauls of up to 20 tons. This was a useful facility for extricating lighter vehicles when a straight rear pull was impracticable; for instance, a vehicle that had run off the road could be recovered by such means without the ARV having to straddle the road and thereby disrupt traffic. Similarly, fairleads and pulley guides were fitted to the roof of the vehicle to enable front pulls and self-recovery to be achieved. Pushing of casualties was sometimes necessary, and for this purpose a wooden bumper bar was used. To provide a safe seating for this a square socket was mounted on the lower front hull plate.

A two-piece aluminium jib cable capable of a 10-ton lift, sufficient to remove the turret of a Centurion gun tank, could be mounted on the front of the hull. When this was in use the vehicle had only limited ability to manoeuvre backwards and forwards, as any turns induced the load to swing and led to distortion or collapse of the jib. Provision was made for mounting an 'A'-frame jib on the ground anchor with a lifting capacity of 30 tons, or 12 tons when folded for towing. Neither of these devices found favour with the British Army, and they were rarely fitted. The stowage of the front jib on the vehicle so reduced space for ancillary recovery equipment that it was more often than not discarded. Towing was normally achieved by means of 'A'-frame Hollebone bars capable of pulling even the heaviest vehicles in service. Extensive recovery equipment was carried in stowage bins extending to the top of the winch compartment and in smaller bins on the front plate of the superstructure. Stowage bins and baskets were mounted over the rear trackguards and exhaust silencers for miscellaneous items such as gun planks, pusher bars and ground anchors. The right-hand side trackguard bin had internal fittings to carry oxyacetylene gas cylinders for welding and cutting – especially useful for cutting thrown tracks. Vehicle armament consisted of one 0.30in Browning MG mounted on the

commander's No 1 Mark 2 cupola for air and ground defence. An auxiliary 102-gallon fuel tank was housed in the front left compartment of the hull where, on the gun tank, the forward 20-round ammunition bin and water tank were situated. This did much to alleviate the limited operational range of the vehicle, but even so, fuel consumption when towing a casualty was commonly of the order of 5 gallons per mile (in the jungles of Vietnam, under particularly difficult conditions, the Australians recorded consumptions of 15 gallons per mile).

The first prototype vehicle was built by Garner Motors of Acton. The design incorporated a winch generator coupled to an electric winch motor made by Crompton Parkinson of Chelmsford, which had been originally developed as a trolleybus motor for a Toronto omnibus company. Prototype 00ZR63 was completed on New Year's Eve 1952 and underwent trials from February 1953 until July 1954. Early winch drums tended to distort, but this was corrected by strengthening with internal ribs. Other problems included inadequate cooling of the auxiliary engine and deflection of the winch under heavy loads. Once these had been satisfactorily resolved, production began in 1955 at Vickers-Armstrongs and ROF Woolwich Arsenal. The majority were conversions of existing vehicles, although a number were built on new Centurion Mark 5 hulls. The prototype and first production vehicle were tested between May 1955 and May 1956.

The Centurion ARV Mark 2 entered service with the British Army in 1956, and was employed extensively around the world. Manned by REME personnel, four ARVs were attached to each armoured regiment of the RAC, one for each sabre squadron and one in regimental headquarters. Many unofficial modifications were made by recovery mechanics during its long career, including the mounting of two headlights on the trackguards in place of the central lights on the glacis plate. The two rear-mounted searchlight sockets were adapted to accept two more boiling vessels for cooking and washing. A penthouse, usually the canvas tilt of a 3-tonner, was erected over the rear hull section for living accommodation. With the aforementioned cooking vessels, the heat from the auxiliary charging engine and a portable

ABOVE The Centurion ARV Mark 2 saw widespread employment worldwide from Suez to South Vietnam, remaining in active service until after the 1991 Gulf War. REME recovery mechanics (or 'reccy mechs') were adept at making themselves comfortable in the field. It was standard practice to acquire the canvas tilt and stanchions from a '3-tonner' to act as shelter over the rear of the vehicle, providing a warm sleeping area at night. The number Eight denoted REME and thus this ARV was attached to C Squadron.

BELOW The design of a definitive ARV based on the Centurion began in 1951, entering service as the Centurion ARV Mark 2 in 1956. It was issued on a scale of four per armoured regiment, with one in each squadron within the REME Light Aid Detachment (LAD).

television set run off the vehicle's batteries, 'recy mechs' were the envy of tank crews during exercises in the depths of a German winter. By virtue of the fact that there were no hydraulic systems in the design it was commendably reliable and popular with its crews but, as with all vehicles, there were a number of unfavourable features. The radio operator, who sat on top of the B80 engine with only 2ft 6in of headroom when closed down, was particularly uncomfortable. The commander's field of vision in such circumstances was very limited due to the centre channel running along the roof of the vehicle. One disadvantage was that in order to deploy the winch ropes the ARV had to reverse as close as possible to the casualty, attach the rope and then move forward to pay out the required length of rope. If the casualty was bogged in marshy ground, the ARV could not approach too close for fear of bogging itself, so the crew were obliged to hand-haul the rope – a laborious and unwelcome task. The winch operator was so situated that he was often unable to see the casualty, and all signals had to be relayed to him by the commander via the remote intercom. A Centurion ARV Mark 3 was proposed to overcome these problems, with a forward crew compartment and the ability for front recovery similar to Conqueror ARV Mark 2, but it never proceeded beyond a design study. A further proposal to build the ARV on a Mark 7 hull also never came to fruition.

One interesting variant that did enter service was the Centurion ARV Mark 2 Spare Barrel Carrier. In 1962 many ARVs in BAOR were modified to carry two 105mm gun barrels along the trackguards in place of the side stowage bins. The intention was to provide the sabre squadrons with ready replacements of gun barrels once they had been 'shot out' in battle. Due to the lack of lifting equipment in forward areas, and the limitation of vehicle stowage space, they were disliked by REME crews and the majority were subsequently reconverted to their original configuration. The Centurion ARV Mark 2 proved to be an extremely effective vehicle. It was employed in combat at Suez, by the Israelis, and in South Vietnam with the Australians. The ARV Mark 2 was withdrawn from front-line service with the armoured regiments of BAOR in 1979.

Centurion Mark 5 Dozer (FV4019)

The Tank, Gun, Centurion Mark 5, Dozer was a Rhine Army conversion of a standard Mark 5 gun tank fitted with a hydraulically operated dozer blade and ancillary equipment. Tankdozers are employed for a variety of tasks on the battlefield, including the digging of tank scrapes for hull-down fire positions, route clearance through devastated towns, filling in anti-tank ditches and other minor earth-moving work. Centurion Tankdozers entered service with the RAC in 1961, and were usually issued on a scale of one per squadron.

The dozer blade, manufactured by T.B. Pearsons Limited of Newcastle, was identical to that fitted to the Centurion AVRE. Features of the blade included a renewable steel bottom cutting edge, and a hinged flap at the top. The flap hung down by reason of its weight until scooped spoil lifted it, thereby increasing the effective depth of the blade. Reducing the normal height of the blade in this way avoided the bottom edge being so low that it affected the vehicle's ability to negotiate obstacles. Nor did it obscure the driver's vision during travelling; as the blade filled, the flap came into the driver's view, and was a valuable indication of blade load. The dozer blade was controlled by a joystick in the driver's compartment, and the system operated by means of a hydraulic pump driven by the main engine, designated the Meteor Mark 4B-H (the suffix H denoting the modifications made to the standard engine to drive the hydraulic pump). The hydraulic system and pumps were designed and manufactured by H.M. Hobson Limited of Wolverhampton. As with all hydraulic systems, constant skilled maintenance was necessary to ensure reliability. When properly serviced, the Centurion Dozer performed well in its many tasks.

The designation of most Centurion variants was based on the mark number of the original vehicle; as the conversions were carried out on Mark 5 gun tanks, the tankdozers were designated Centurion Mark 5 Dozers. The dozer attachment made the vehicles nose-heavy and precluded the fitting of appliqué

ABOVE The Centurion Mark 5 Dozer was a standard gun tank fitted with a hydraulically operated blade. It was usually issued on a scale of one per sabre squadron within armoured regiments for such earthmoving tasks as digging tank scrapes for hull-down positions. The dozer blade controls were operated by the driver using a joystick like his gear-change lever. It was the same equipment as fitted to the Centurion Mark 5 Armoured Vehicle Royal Engineers (AVRE).

armour to the glacis plate, as was done with gun tanks which, following uparmouring, became Centurion Mark 5/1s. The majority of these gun tanks were subsequently upgunned with 105mm guns to become Mark 6s, and later, with the installation of ranging guns and IR night-fighting equipment, Mark 11s. The fitting of 105mm guns to tankdozers changed their designation to Centurion Mark 5/2 Dozer, following the standard system. The installation of a ranging gun to these vehicles produced a hybrid mark, the Mark 5/3, as no British Army gun tanks were used in this configuration. Thus the Mark 5/3 was a basic Mark 5 that had been upgunned and fitted with a ranging gun without having been uparmoured first. In the British Army only tankdozers were so designated, but the Dutch Army employed gun tanks modified to this configuration with the addition of IR night-fighting equipment. Tankdozers were exported to several foreign users of the Centurion, including Australia and Denmark.

This sequence of photographs shows the launching of the Bridge Tank No 6 by a Centurion bridgelayer, a process that took approximately 90 seconds under ideal conditions and two minutes to recover the bridge. It was a distinct tactical advantage to be able to recover the bridge from either end to maintain the momentum of an advance across multiple obstacles.

Centurion Bridgelayer Mark 5 (FV4002)

The Centurion Bridgelayer was used for carrying and launching a single-span bridge across rivers and gaps up to 45ft wide. It was fully armoured and normally used in the assault phase of a crossing, the bridge being laid in less than 2 minutes without exposure of the crew to enemy fire. The design of a tank-mounted bridgelayer to replace the wartime Churchill type began in 1946 at MEXE (Military Engineering Experimental Establishment) Christchurch in conjunction with FVRDE, and was originally intended for the FV200 series universal tank. In late 1946 a steel lattice framework was built atop an A41 prototype (P3) to prove the feasibility of utilising a vehicle 52ft in length. With the demise of the FV200, the project proceeded at a low priority. A mock-up bridge was fitted to a Centurion Mark 1 hull in 1952, to test performance at the projected battle weight of 49 tons 2cwt; development continued slowly, and it was not until 1956 that an operational prototype was produced based on a Centurion Mark 7 chassis, built by Hudswell Clark Limited of Leeds. User trials of the bridgelayer, together with a second prototype vehicle built to production standards, were completed by September 1958. These trials proved the feasibility of the concept, but it was decided to base the production version on redundant Mark 5 hulls. This caused considerable delays due to the many differences of detail between the two chassis.

The first pre-production Bridgelayer Mark 5 was completed at ROF Barnbow in early 1960. Acceptance trials were conducted between June and September of that year, and production began in 1961. The production contract for the British Army was completed in 1963 but further models were built at Barnbow for foreign customers until 1966. A reworked prototype bridgelayer was delivered to Bovington in April 1962 for instructional training. Production versions entered service with the RAC and RE in 1963.

The basis of the Centurion Bridgelayer Mark 5 was a conversion of a Centurion Mark 5 hull reworked to the latest automotive standards and with the Centurion Mark 7's electrical system. The turret, gun control equipment, ammunition bins and ancillaries were discarded, and a hull roof plate was fitted over the turret ring; this incorporated an access hatch for the wireless operator, and air inlet and outlet louvres for the B40 engine. Behind the operator's hatch was an aerial tower which could be elevated in order to raise the aerial tuning unit and aerial above the level of the bridge when stowed. A second aerial tower was mounted on the rear bridge support structure. The bridge launching mechanism was operated by a Tower hydraulic pump driven by means of a propeller shaft from a Rolls-Royce B40 No 1 Mark 5P petrol engine located in the fighting compartment beside the wireless operator. The commander sat alongside the driver in the position formerly occupied by the 20-round ammunition bin and water tank. He had a simple rotatable cupola with three periscopes, incorporating mounting lugs for a machine gun – the only armament carried apart from the crew's small arms. The vehicle was fitted with a pair of smoke dischargers mounted on the front bridge support structure. A 100-gallon auxiliary fuel tank was mounted on the rear hull plate to extend the radius of action.

The Bridge Tank No 6 was of aluminium alloy riveted-plate girder construction and comprised four identical quarter trackways, each 26ft long and 5ft 8.5in wide. Each quarter section could be transported by a 3-ton truck. The quarters were joined together in pairs

ABOVE A pair of Centurions cross a Tank Bridge No 6 under the watchful eye of a sapper. At the outset three Centurion bridgelayers were issued to each armoured regiment but their great bulk and length meant they were rarely taken on exercise and so became something of a liability. Once all bridgelayers were centralised in the Armoured Engineer Squadrons of the Royal Engineers they became much more effective in the field as brigade asset.

to form two trackways each 52ft long. The vehicle was provided with a lifting jib attached to the launching arm to assemble the four quarter sections to make a complete bridge. It could not, however, lift the 7-ton bridge when assembled and, being somewhat limited in application, it was only used when more suitable lifting tackle was unavailable (although it did prove useful for other tasks, including track maintenance). Each trackway was connected together by means of two portal frames and a diagonal brace, giving a longitudinal gap 2ft 6in wide between the tracks. Lifting brackets were fitted to each trackway and were engaged by the bridgelayer launching arm, enabling the bridge to be laid or recovered from either end. The steel portal frames were sufficiently strong to support the weight of each trackway during launching, but were intended to bend under the load imposed by a heavy vehicle crossing the bridge when it rested on uneven ground. Two spare portal frames were supplied with each bridgelayer to replace those distorted during bridging operations. The bridge classification was Class 80.

The launching mechanism comprised a launching arm, roller frame, upper cylinder and lower cylinder, attached to a triangular supporting structure welded to the hull glacis plate. The controls of the B40 engine and hydraulic pump unit to actuate the launching mechanism were located in the co-driver's compartment and were operated by the commander. At approximately the centre of its length, the upper cylinder was attached to, and was free to pivot about, the apex of the triangular supporting structure. The free end of the upper cylinder piston rod was connected to the launching arm. The roller frame was also attached to, and was free to pivot about, the apex of the supporting structure. The launching arm, which fitted into the central gap between the two trackways of the bridge, had projecting bosses on each side, both near the base and at the free end. These bosses engaged with inverted U-blocks attached to the girders of the bridge. Automatically operated sliding pins were fitted coaxially in the centre of each boss; these pins were retracted inside the bosses when the bridge was fully launched, thus allowing the launching arm to fall free of the inverted

U-blocks, but when recovering the bridge the pins were projected from the bosses and, before the bridge was vertical, they engaged with holes in the bridge girders. This prevented the bridge falling off the launching arm as it passed over the vertical and was coming down into its travelling position on top of the tank (a spectacular and disconcerting phenomenon that happened on more than one occasion when the pins failed to engage properly). The lower cylinder was attached at one end of a pivot on the nose of the tank and the free end of the piston rod was attached to the roller frame.

In the travelling position the bridge was carried on the sliding pins of the launching arm and laid upside-down on rubber blocks on the rear support structure, where it was securely held by two clamps during cross-country driving. Before launching it was essential to release these clamps, but in action it was possible to effect this with built-in explosive charges. In order to launch the bridge, the operator opened the solenoid-controlled valves that directed the flow of oil from the oil pump driven by the B40 engine to the annulus of both cylinders. Since the piston of the upper cylinder was fully retracted, no movement of this piston rod occurred, but the piston rod of the lower cylinder retracted, thereby rotating the roller frame, the upper cylinder and the launching arm, and hence the bridge about the common centre of the apex of the supporting structure. This motion continued until the bridge was vertical, when limit switches changed over the solenoid-operated control valves and oil was then directed to the annulus of the lower cylinder and the rear end of the upper cylinder. This held the piston rod of the lower cylinder in the fully retracted position and extended the piston rod of the upper cylinder, thereby rotating the launching arm about the centre of the rollers and lowering the bridge to the ground. When the bridge was fully launched, the launching arm was allowed to continue its rotation until it was clear of the inverted U-blocks, when the motion was stopped by the operator. The tank then reversed clear of the bridge.

It will be evident that when the bridge was being lowered from the vertical position to the ground it would, if not restricted, fall freely under its own weight. The speed of descent was controlled by a special valve which was so arranged that the launching arm was actually forced down by the pump. Thus the speed of operation was directly proportional to the speed of the pump, which was under the control of the operator throughout the entire cycle. For recovery, the cycle was the same as above but in reverse. The whole bridgelaying sequence took less time than it does to read this passage; the total launch time was 100 seconds, while recovery could be achieved in 2 minutes under favourable conditions. The bridge could be launched on a cross slope of 1 in 10, with a maximum permissible fore and aft tilt of 1 in 4, and between banks having an 8ft difference in height on a clear span of 45ft. Centre decking sections were provided to allow passage of Centurion gun tanks towing mono-wheel fuel trailers. (It was not unknown for a Centurion to drag its trailer between the trackways rather than lift and shackle it to the rear hull plate, the previously prescribed method.) The centre decking also prevented small-wheeled vehicles and marching troops from falling into the gap between the trackways. The sections were stowed on the bazooka plates, rear fuel tank and transmission covers when not in use. Luminous discs, known by the grandiose title of 'luminary assemblies', were fitted to the top edges of the kerbs and in the bridge inner slots to facilitate night crossings. The bridgelayer could be employed for 'overbridging' weak or damaged bridges that were unable to bear the weight of AFVs. By laying the No 6 Tank Bridge on chocks at either end, it was possible for even the heaviest vehicles to negotiate flimsy bridges that would otherwise have impeded the advance.

Centurion Bridgelayers were originally issued to the RAC on the scale of three to a regiment, one to each sabre squadron. However, their great height and inability to negotiate the narrow streets of many German towns and villages meant that they were unable to keep up with the gun tanks, and it was often necessary to reconnoitre a special route for them to bypass obstacles such as low bridges and power cables. This, together with the problems encountered with the complex hydraulic system and a shortage of spare parts, made them somewhat unpopular with the Armoured Corps.

Often they were off the road, and remained behind at barracks to be cannibalised as spare parts for the gun tanks. All bridgelayers were subsequently transferred to the Royal Engineers to become part of the Armoured Engineer Squadrons. Once under centralised control it was possible to devote more attention to their upkeep, and they proved to be most effective in their tasks.

Centurion Beach Armoured Recovery Vehicle (BARV) (FV4018)

The primary role of the Beach Armoured Recovery Vehicle (BARV) is to effect the recovery of drowned vehicles to the shoreline and maintain exits from landing craft clear during assault landings. It can also push off stranded landing craft mechanised (LCM) by means of its nosing block and drag broached landing craft vehicle and personnel (LCVP) into deep water. It is employed for many other general tasks on the assault beach, such as laying flexible trackways and on more than one occasion has been used as a temporary anchorage for small craft.

During the 1950s the only vehicle available to fill this requirement was the wartime Sherman BARV. Although it had given admirable service in its day, spares for the Sherman BARV were in short supply and, since it was inclined to float in 8ft of water, it was unable to retrieve the heavier armoured vehicles then entering

BELOW The Centurion Beach Armoured Recovery Vehicle (BARV) was designed for a very specific purpose as its name implies. Just 12 BARVs were made at ROF Barnbow and they served first with the REME and then with the Royal Marines during amphibious landings.

ABOVE BARV 06BA34 undertakes a typical recovery task of a Centurion ARV Mark 2. The BARV had no winching equipment and relied on tractive effort to push or pull vehicles stranded on the beach or in the shallows. Similarly it used its front 'nosing' block to push beached landing craft back into open water. Of interest, the Centurion ARV Mark 2 in the background is configured for deep wading with the driver's capsule resting on the vehicle roof.

service. MTDE Technical Group REME, Fording Trials, located at Instow in North Devon (subsequently Fording Trials Branch (FTB)), were tasked with the design and building of a mock-up vehicle to replace the Sherman. In January 1957, a Centurion Tower was delivered to FTB and detailed design and development was undertaken. The hull was gutted of all equipment and assemblies except for the engine, clutch and gearbox, while the general layout of the driver's compartment remained intact. This, coupled with the basic hull design, determined the superstructure, which was shaped to form a bow or cutwater.

The prototype (06ZR24) was constructed of ³⁄₁₆th inch mild steel bolted to a girder framework and made its first dip in June 1957. After further modification it was successfully demonstrated on Instow beach on 4 and 5 March 1958. The prototype then went to FVRDE for final development of the armoured version prior to a production contract for 12 vehicles at ROF Barnbow, Leeds. In February 1960 the first production Centurion BARV arrived at Instow for User trials, which proved it more than adequate for its role. Minor improvements were incorporated and modifications implemented. Production of the 12 vehicles based on Centurion Mark 3 hulls was completed in 1963.

The Centurion BARV had a superstructure of 1in armour plate. The vehicle was able to wade in up to 9ft 6in of water, although the usual maximum operating depth is 8ft. In water less than 5ft deep, the driver had direct vision

through a laminated glass block, but in greater depths he was directed by the commander from the opened hatch. This single hatch gave access to the working compartment for all crew members. The BARV had a crew of four including the commander, driver/radio operator and two recovery mechanics, one of whom was a trained diver. His tasks included working in water up to 20ft in depth to attach tow ropes to casualties and to cut away with oxyacetylene equipment any obstruction impeding recovery, such as wreckage or beach obstacles entangled with the tracks. Two types of diving equipment were used; one utilised pure oxygen, the other compressed air. As the BARV operated on soft ground or in water where the effective weight could be as low as 15 tons, all shock absorbers were removed to reduce servicing. The probability of enemy ground attack by rocket launchers was discounted and in any case the best defence against any attack, be it from ground or air, was to position the BARV in deep water. In consequence the bazooka plates were discarded, much to the approval of BARV crews. To achieve continuous wading up to its maximum depth presented problems of refuelling, engine air intake and dispersal of exhaust fumes. The fuelling problem was solved by installing an 85-gallon fuel tank in the original hull air outlet grille box together with an external watertight filler cap. The silencers were positioned on top of the superstructure air outlet grille and, by altering the engine exhaust manifolds, the complete exhaust system was installed inside the vehicle without intricate plumbing. Air supply to the engine was ducted via armoured cowls behind the commander's hatch through air cleaners located in the crew compartment to simplify servicing. The cumulative effect of removing fuel tanks, relocating the exhaust system and discarding the auxiliary engine produced an engine compartment with all assemblies readily accessible. The BARV carried its own lifting tackle which, when not in use, was stowed on brackets attached to the superstructure sides. The lifting gantry with a 1-ton Morris block could be erected in an hour by three men and by unbolting the rear door, the engine, clutch or gearbox could be lifted out with relative ease. The BARV crew were capable of carrying out all these tasks either on board ship, weather permitting, or in the field.

The normal trackguards were replaced by heavy wire mesh catwalks through which water passed freely to reduce buoyancy. Three handrail guards were fitted at the front. These were painted white, as were all attachment points in order to aid location by the driver when working submerged in conditions of low visibility. Various items of stowage were attached to the superstructure walls including spare roadwheels, pioneer tools, fire extinguishers and towing hawsers. The BARV had no winching equipment but 2:1 pulls could be achieved using the snatchblock, which was stowed above the driver's compartment. Normal recovery was achieved by straight towing. Tractive effort on dry land was 28 tons, which reduced by 2 tons for every foot of water. The front fender could also be used for recovery of casualties by pushing them to dry land. A front stowage bin was located behind the fender, housing materials not unduly susceptible to damage by immersion in water.

Communications were provided by two wireless sets, C42 and B47, though a third radio A43 was often carried for BARV for short communication. Besides the normal crew IC system, a 'Transhailer' was provided for direct 'loudspeaker' communication with the crew. Because of the reduced electrical requirement of the BARV, the auxiliary generator was replaced by a modified 'Chore-Horse' 300W 24V charging unit. Armament comprised one GPMG and a Sterling sub-machine gun for each crew member. Despite constant use, the BARVs clocked up only low mileages, the reason for this being that they operated more often in reverse gear, which was not recorded on the odometer. At 40 tons, the BARV was the fastest Centurion on dry land. With the usual tuning and isolating of the governors by REME personnel, speeds in excess of 30mph were achieved.

The BARV saw extensive service with the British Army manned by REME personnel, notably with the Royal Navy Amphibious Warfare Squadron in the Middle East. The BARV was normally the first vehicle to be disembarked on a landing to keep beach channels clear of drowned and stationary vehicles. Recovery in support of beach landings was undertaken by BARV working in conjunction with a Michigan Light-Wheeled Tractor to form an 'amphibious beach unit'. Two such units, together with one Size 2 Dozer, two 3-tonners and two Land Rovers formed the Army Beach Troop Royal Engineers – a true combined arms operation. With the withdrawal of the British Army from east of Suez, assault landings have become the preserve of the Royal Marines and they became the main users of the Centurion BARV. The two LPDs (landing platform dock) HMS *Fearless* and HMS *Intrepid* each carried one BARV crewed by Royal Marines. Operating in conjunction with other Navy and RAF support, the LPDs carried all types of military equipment, including tanks, to effect an amphibious landing anywhere within NATO. To this end the BARVs were modified for use in winter operations in Norway. Both *Fearless* and *Intrepid* and one BARV were involved in the landings in 1982 at San Carlos Bay during the Falklands War. The last BARV to see active service was 02ZR77 in 2003 during the Second Gulf War. Thereafter the Centurion BARV was superseded by the Hippo, based on the chassis of a Leopard 1.

Centurion Armoured Vehicle Royal Engineers (AVRE) Mark 5 (FV4003)

The Centurion AVRE was the workhorse of the armoured engineers. It was designed to undertake a number of roles on the battlefield. It mounted a large-calibre, low-velocity demolition gun to destroy defended strongpoints and pillboxes. The vehicle could launch a fascine into a gap to enable armoured vehicles to cross streams, trenches and anti-tank ditches. A dozer blade was fitted for improving crossing places, clearing rubble and other similar tasks. Development of the Centurion AVRE began in 1953 at FVRDE to replace the Churchill AVRE Mark VII that had entered service in 1954. Initial trials were held to prove whether the Centurion was able to carry a fascine, which it did with no apparent damage to the front suspension units. The War Office approved the basic design in July 1955 and the prototype vehicle was delivered to FVRDE in August 1957. The AVRE was a modified Centurion Mark 5 gun tank with

ABOVE AND BELOW The fascine is an ancient military device used for a host of purposes, but in modern times is used primarily for filling anti-tank ditches to allow the passage of AFVs across the obstacle. Fascines were first used in conjunction with tanks during the First World War, notably at the Battle of Cambrai in November 1917. It comprises bundles of brushwood bound together to form a gap-crossing device. Weighing six to seven tons and an extra ton when wet, a brushwood fascine also had the effect of damming when used in a ditch or waterway. Accordingly, the Royal Engineers developed the Max-Pipe Fascine comprising lengths of PVC piping that weighed only two tons, thus exerting less wear and tear on the carrying vehicle; it also allows water to pass through freely without damming. The two types of fascine are shown on these Centurion AVREs.

an Ordnance B.L. 165mm (6.5in) AVRE L9A1 firing a powerful projectile with accuracy up to 2,000yd. The 64lb demolition charge projectile contained 31lb 13oz 7 drams of PE4 explosive, equivalent to six rounds of 120mm HESH ammunition. Its accuracy was such that bridge girders could be destroyed at 600yd, bridge piers and pillboxes at 1,400yd and at greater ranges it served as an effective area weapon. The AVRE mounted a hydraulically operated dozer blade, identical to that of the Centurion Mark 5 Tankdozer, with an output capacity of 30cu yd per hour. It was used for a multitude of tasks, such as route clearance in built-up areas and woods, route denial, creating or filling anti-tank ditches, improving bridge approaches and river crossing points and digging gun emplacements and tank slots. As an indication of its effectiveness, the AVRE was able to dig a hull-down fire position for a gun tank in light soil within 7 minutes. The dozer could also be used as a grader by 'back-blading', to smooth the ground before laying metal Class 60 Trackway. The latter was a most versatile device that had many uses such as a bridge approach, helicopter landing pad, recovery base on boggy ground, riverbank exit and entry and as a tank slewing pad. It was carried on a cradle mounted over the glacis plate and deployed by means of three explosive 'blow-out' pins;

one was fired to release the trackway from the cradle and the other two to drop it once it had been laid in position. The whole operation was controlled from under armour without exposure of the crew.

The cradle was also used to carry a fascine that could be launched into gaps of up to 20ft wide. This ancient technique of warfare was a staple but highly effective means of trench crossing that has been used by British tanks since the First World War. It consisted of a bundle of brushwood or chestnut stakes fashioned into a cylindrical bundle 8–10ft in diameter by 16ft long and weighing 5–8 tons depending on the water content. It was usually bound around a number of steel tubes, often scaffolding, to allow water to flow through in order to prevent damming and consequential flooding of a crossing place. The fascine was jettisoned either manually or by electrically fired 'blow-out' pins. With the fascine in the cradle, vehicle speed was limited to 10mph and the commander was obliged to ride on a seat atop the turret to guide the driver. This precarious perch was used only infrequently as the driver had sufficient limited forward vision below the cradle. Before the advent of Class 30 and Class 60 Trackway, it was standard practice to split the fascine to form a roadway approximately 50ft in length over muddy ground. The

ABOVE AND BELOW The Centurion Mark 5 AVRE was the successor to the Churchill AVREs that had originated during the Second World War with the 79th Armoured Division. The vehicle configuration was much the same with a fascine cradle at the front mounted above the driver's compartment and a powerful demolition gun in the turret in place of the standard main armament. The original Centurion AVRE embodied a 165mm demolition gun for the destruction of field fortifications such as pillboxes and other well-entrenched positions. The AVRE also incorporated a front-mounted dozer blade for a multitude of earthmoving tasks on the battlefield with a capacity of 300cu yd/hr. Subsequently the Royal Engineers employed standard gun tanks as well, designated Centurion 105 AVRE, and the former type Centurion 165 AVRE (as shown above).

LEFT This series of photographs shows the deployment of a Pipe Fascine by a Centurion 165 AVRE into an anti-tank ditch. The technique is to approach the obstacle at speed and then brake suddenly at the same moment as firing the explosive bolts retaining the fascine in the cradle. The inertia propels the fascine forward into the ditch and the AVRE then crosses its own fascine to continue the advance.

prototype AVRE was fitted with a hydraulic 1¾-ton winch on the rear hull which served to parbuckle or pull the fascine on to the cradle by means of a six-part line. The prototype also had a mounting on the glacis plate for a 10-ton jib, similar to that of the ARV Mark 2, which, in conjunction with the winch, was intended to lift engineering equipment or clear obstacles.

It proved to be too unwieldy in practice and neither device was fitted to production vehicles. The AVRE could haul a 7½-ton four-wheel trailer designed to carry a fascine, Class 60 Trackway roll, demolition stores or other sapper equipment. The AVRE trailer could be jettisoned at will by firing an explosive release mechanism in the rotatable towing hook. It could traverse any terrain negotiable by the AVRE without seriously reducing the performance of the towing vehicle. The AVRE could also tow two Barmine mechanical minelayers – either singly or in pairs – behind the trailer for rapid minelaying operations. The trailer could carry 864 mines in pallets compared with 144 in a conventional FV432 APC. One other trailer designed for use with AVRE was the Giant Viper anti-tank mine clearing equipment. This device was used to blast a passage for tanks and vehicles through a minefield up to 600ft in depth. A development of the wartime Conger, it consisted of 750ft of 2⅝in-diameter hose filled with plastic explosive mounted on a two-wheeled trailer. In use, the AVRE towing the equipment halted approximately 150ft from the edge of a minefield and the Giant Viper was fired from within the vehicle. It was projected across the minefield by a cluster of eight rocket motors.

The tail end of the hose was fitted with arrester gear in the form of three parachutes, which straightened the hose during flight and operated the striker mechanism to detonate

RIGHT AND CENTRE Both types of Centurion AVRE are capable of hauling trailers especially designed for Royal Engineers including the 7½-ton four-wheel trailer (shown at top) to carry such stores as Class 60 Trackway; No 7 Anti-Tank Mines; an extra fascine or crates of RDD explosives. The second trailer is designed to carry the Giant Viper anti-tank mine clearing equipment.

the charge on landing. Performance was dependent upon a number of factors but Giant Viper could be expected to render inoperative a high percentage of blast susceptible anti-tank and anti-personnel mines over a pathway 24ft wide by 600ft long. Besides the fascine cradle, dozer blade and demolition gun, other modifications to the basic Centurion Mark 5 included greater fuel capacity with an additional 100-gallon fuel tank in an armoured downward extension of the hull rear, revised cooling air outlets above the transmission compartment and an additional crew member alongside the driver. The communication system included VHF radio consisting of B47 and C42 wireless sets. One of each was fitted in a troop AVRE and an additional C42 in a command AVRE.

IR equipment could be fitted for night-driving and -fighting. User trials of the Centurion AVRE began in February 1962 and it entered service with the Royal Engineers in 1963. It formed the basic equipment of the three Armoured Engineer Squadrons of 32nd Assault Engineer Regiment in Germany. Originally each squadron consisted of three armoured troops, each of three AVREs and two Centurion Bridgelayers and a troop of four Centurion ARKs. Later the composition varied and became more flexible to suit the tactical situation at hand. The British Army was the only force to use the Centurion AVRE and it was employed operationally in Northern Ireland and the Gulf. In 1972, four Centurion AVREs were used to remove the reinforced barricades in the so-called 'no-go' area of the Creggan estate in Londonderry during the opening phase of Operation Motorman. About 20-odd years later the AVREs were employed to clear the Basra road of wreckage in a task nicknamed Operation Motorman 2, with one AVRE being involved in both operations.

BELOW Although the Centurion 165 AVRE was the workhorse of the Armoured Engineers, the Centurion 105 AVRE became the specialised anti-tank minefield clearing variant since it was impractical to fit a fascine cradle on this version. It fires the rocket-propelled Giant Viper that blasts a passage for vehicles through a minefield up to 200yd wide. To ensure that all mines have been eliminated, the AVRE then uses its Track Width Mine Plough (shown here) to negotiate the same path so that any unexploded mines or those not susceptible to blast over-pressure are disinterred and discarded to each side.

Centurion Armoured Ramp Carrier (ARK) (FV4016)

The role of the Centurion ARK was the rapid assault bridging of shallow gaps of up to 75ft wide and of high banks. The vehicle itself entered the obstacle and acted as a central pier. Development of the Centurion single ARK began in 1958 under the design parentage of FVRDE. It comprised a standard Centurion Mark 5 from which the turret was removed. Modifications to the hull were of a minor nature. An armoured plate covered the turret ring. A simple commander's cupola was positioned alongside the driver with a conning tower behind to enable the driver to be directed during wading operations. Wading screen frames were fitted around the engine and transmission covers which differed from those of a standard gun tank as the trackways fouled the normal type. The main and auxiliary engine exhaust pipes were extended to permit wading to a depth of 8ft. Four banks of six-barrel smoke dischargers were fitted below the level of the trackways, two on each side of the front of the vehicle. The total of 24 barrels – 12 of which faced forwards and 12 sideways – created a quick and effective smokescreen to mask the vehicle during bridging operations. A robust superstructure of six posts, surmounted by three cross-bearers, supported two longitudinal decks at each end of which was attached a folding ramp, consisting of main, centre and tail sections. The ramps could be extended mechanically to form, in conjunction with two centre decks, a roadway over 80ft long with an effective horizontal span

of 75ft when a bank setting of 2ft 6in at each end was used. The decks were located at each side of the vehicle leaving a central gap. A screw mechanism at each end of the superstructure provided a means of varying the distance by which the decks and ramps were separated. The innermost position reduced the overall width of the vehicle for transportation purposes, while the extreme outer location permitted passage of the largest vehicles up to Class 80. In this position the centre gap was too wide to permit the passage of small vehicles and centre docking sections were provided for this purpose, a laborious and disagreeable task for the three-man crew. The hull was fitted with stabilising jacks at front and rear. Power for extending the ramps was provided by a hydraulic pump mounted on and driven by the main engine.

This operated the ram of a centrally mounted vertical hydraulic jack which, when extended, pulled steel wire cables to raise the main section of the ramp to the vertical position. A second steel wire rope system controlled the centre and tail sections until they were aligned at approximately 45 degrees. This was the launching position from which actuation of a release lever in the crew compartment dropped the ramps. Expendable crusher boxes (often empty 5-gallon oil drums) were attached to the underside of the tail section of the ramps to absorb the impact on landing. The trackways could be launched prior to entering, or in the gap, depending on the nature of the banks. Recovery of the ramps, a long and arduous task, necessitated the use of two vehicles in conjunction with a recovery strut and sling.

BELOW The Centurion ARK, or Armoured Ramp Carrier, was another legacy of the 79th Armoured Division in the Second World War, designed for breaching sea walls during an assault landing such as was done on D-Day in 1944. It also acted as a bridgelayer for crossing waterways when it entered the obstacle and acted as a central pier. In this capacity the ARK had an effective span of 75ft, capable of bearing the largest vehicles in service.

Built at RAF Barnbow, the ARK entered service with the Royal Engineers in 1965. Together with the Centurion AVRE and Centurion Bridgelayer, it served with the assault engineers of the 2nd, 26th and 31st Armoured Engineer Regiments. Each squadron had four ARKs that, together with two AVREs, usually formed the 3rd Troop.

Besides spanning wide gaps the ARK was capable of launching its ramps over walls and earthworks up to 19ft in height to give means of crossing. It was employed during river crossings as an exit over high-sided banks for wading tanks, a manoeuvre that required skilled driving to enable the tanks to negotiate the submerged ramps. In similar circumstances, the ARK was used as an unloading pier at riverbanks.

One interesting variant of the ARK was the CAMP – Centurion ARK Mobile Pier. Experience of operating the ARK had shown that when it was employed in the conventional mode as a bridge across a water-filled obstacle, it acted as a dam to the flow of water, creating scouring and build-up of the river bed. On occasions this caused the vehicle to tilt and when vehicles crossed the bridge resulted in distortion of the ramps. To overcome this problem a number of ARKs had their folding ramps removed, leaving only the central trackways. The CAMP was driven into the river and placed in the centre parallel to the banks. The vehicle was then used as a stepping-stone for two No 6 Tank Bridges. One Centurion Bridgelayer deployed its bridge from the nearside bank on to the CAMP. The second Bridgelayer mounted the first Tank Bridge and laid its own on to the further bank. On one occasion a river crossing was achieved by employing two CAMPs and three No 6 Tank Bridges, but the problems of alignment posed considerable difficulties and it was not a technique to be undertaken in the heat of battle. It did, however, prove that it was possible to span wider rivers than those using conventional methods.

The British Army was the only user of the Centurion ARK, a legacy of its wartime experience of employing this unusual and interesting technique of obstacle crossing. The Centurion ARKs were withdrawn from service in 1975. Three vehicles were subsequently utilised at the RE Wing Bovington for driver training. With all trackways and superstructure removed, they were known as Wedges.

ABOVE AND BELOW A Centurion ARK deploys its ramps over a steep embankment, with 'crusher' boxes at the end of each ramp to absorb the impact on landing, followed by a Chieftain Mark 2 as it negotiates the ARK's trackways. Guide markers run along the edge of the trackways but it can be appreciated that the driver has only limited vision at this point.

Chapter Five

Cold War Centurion

During the height of the Cold War the three armoured divisions of BAOR and those of US Army Europe formed the bulwark against the Soviet Union and the Warsaw Pact. Centurion was to the fore all this while as it was in the armies of Denmark, Holland, Sweden and Switzerland.

OPPOSITE For much of the 1950s the Comet was the standard British tank followed by the Centurion Mark 5, shown here with a US M48A1 Patton (left) and a French AMX-13 (right). Arguably, the latter was more suited to street fighting in Berlin than the other two. This Centurion, 12BA08 DISCOVERER, belonged to C Squadron 4 RTR since all their tanks had names beginning with the fourth letter of the alphabet.

Following the Berlin Blockade and the outbreak of the Korean War, the world divided into two mutually antagonistic camps with the North Atlantic Treaty Organization (NATO) led by the United States, and the Warsaw Pact dominated by the USSR. By 1953, the British Army of the Rhine (BAOR) was equipped with three armoured divisions (the 6th, 7th and 11th) which together with the United States Army Europe provided the main bulwark against Communist expansionism in Europe. With the introduction of National Service in 1948, thousands of young British men swelled the ranks of the British Army to provide the essential manpower for the expansion of BAOR, as well as undertaking active service in the Near and Far East. Now fully equipped with Centurion tanks, the three armoured divisions presented a formidable fighting force with a high level of professionalism as exemplified by Trevor Dady of 2nd Royal Tank Regiment. His account of life in a Centurion during the 1950s is a remarkable testament to the tank and the armoured formations that made up BAOR during the Cold War.

'I started my service on Centurion in September 1955 when I was posted to the Second Royal Tank Regiment at Swinton Barracks in Munster, Germany, having completed my basic military training in the Boys'

BELOW CAVALIER is prepared for action during an exercise with the legendary 'Van Doos' or the Royal 22nd Regiment of the Canadian Army on Sennelager Training Area. On the end of the barrel of the 20-pounder gun is an attachment known as the 'Hohne Organ' that simulated the firing of the main armament with exploding thunder-flashes. It was also used unofficially to bombard other tanks and infantry with Compo tins. *(Photo Trevor Dady)*

Squadron RAC in Bovington. My only tank trade at that time was as a wireless operator on No 19 and 88 sets with which Centurion was then fitted. I had also passed a first-class map-reading course, which was to my benefit later. On arrival in my regiment I was appointed as the troop leader's wireless operator in Two Troop, of 'Cyclops' (name of the Squadron) on his Mark 7 Centurion tank. My troop leader was Second Lieutenant Antony Walker. I found that apart from my troop leader, troop sergeant and troop corporal, I was the only other regular soldier in the troop. The remainder were all National Servicemen.

'Probably due to the very fast turnover of National Servicemen and the lack of regular soldiers, I was promoted to lance corporal in May 1956 and then to corporal in September of the same year. Our troop corporal had recently been demobbed, so I was appointed tank commander of the third tank in the troop, which was a Centurion Mark 5. In the spring of 1956, I completed a Regimental D&M (driving and maintenance) course. The indoor instruction was carried out in Swinton Barracks, and the tank driving was done on Dorbaum, which was a little training area just outside Munster. Driving Centurion was great fun but required great skill as the Merritt-Brown "crash gearbox" needed slick actions and different techniques when driving on roads and cross country, from the driver.

'Road driving gear-changes were done using the "double declutch" system when moving the gearstick between gears in quite a slow manner. Cross-country driving needed a far faster method of gear-changing as the tank's forward momentum would drop off immediately the clutch was depressed to change gear. The cross-country method of gear changing was known as "stick-changing" and had to be done at speed. To do this the driver would depress the clutch, move the gearstick to the central position with his right hand, simultaneously giving the left hand steering tiller a very quick flick to the rear as the gearstick passed through the centre of the gate, and letting out the clutch pedal when the required gear had been selected. Flicking the steering tiller momentarily stopped the gears within the gearbox via the transmission steering drums allowing the speedy gear selection.

'In January 1957 I attended and completed the Gunnery Instructors' course at Lulworth. The tank armament covered on the course was Centurion 20-pounder main armament, and the coaxial .30 Browning. Later, when Centurion was being upgunned with the 105mm, gunnery instructors were advised of the changes required in the gunnery techniques. Each tank was issued with a temporary new range scale which had to be overlaid on the 20-pounder range scale on the range drum to the left of the gunner's head. When carrying out annual range practices, and so as not to waste the 20-pounder ammunition that was still in storage, the 105mm gun barrel would be removed from the turret and a 20-pounder barrel inserted in its place. Gun barrel changes only took a few minutes. The 105mm range scale would have to be removed from the drum when firing 20-pounder ammunition. The gunnery techniques for the 20-pounder and 105mm were very similar, so there was no need for any special training. An outsider would not notice any difference, but the commander and gunner would see the difference in the gun performance and results of target strikes. At the conclusion of the range practices, the 105mm range scale and the 105mm gun barrel would be replaced. Eventually, when all the 20-pounder ammunition had been used up and the 20-pounder range scale no longer needed, it was replaced by a new 105mm range drum.

'At this point, having completed all three tank trade training courses, I was fully conversant with all aspects of the Centurion tank and therefore could help other crew members whenever necessary. My commander's training was passed to me by my troop leader and troop sergeant over a period of weeks when on the training areas. In those days there was no such thing as a tank commanders' course; instead one would have to pick up "tank commanding" as quickly as possible from information given to you by other tank commanders. In 1957 my troop sergeant left the regiment and I assumed the role of troop sergeant, still as a corporal. In the same year, my troop leader also left the regiment on an ERE posting and was not replaced owing to the lack of young officers. I therefore, still as a corporal, was commanding the troop in

ABOVE A highlight of the training year in BAOR was the annual firing camp at the Bergen-Hohne ranges on Lüneberg Heath. Here, Centurion Mark 5s, CRECY and CYCLOPS, are loaded on to tank transporters for the journey to Hohne. At this time the three sabre squadrons of 2 RTR were named AJAX, BADGER and CYCLOPS, while Headquarters Squadron was NERO. The tank named CYCLOPS therefore belonged to the squadron commander. *(Photo Trevor Dady)*

BELOW CAVALIER and other Centurions of CYCLOPS Squadron sit atop Diamond T tank transporters manned by the Polish crews of the Mixed Services Organisation RASC during a move to Hohne. Second World War veteran Polish Army crews manned two MSO tank transporter units, 312 and 317. These crews, who lived almost permanently in the back of their Diamond T transporters, were skilled at moving tanks and knew the German countryside intimately. *(Photo Trevor Dady)*

In command at 20

TROOGH *he is only 20, Sergeant T. A. Dady, of Helen, Southampton, already commands one of Britain's Centurion tanks. He entered the Army as a boy soldier when he was 15. In 1955 he was posted to the 2nd Royal Tank Regiment at Munster in Germany, and within three months was promoted Lance Corporal. Within a year he was promoted Corporal and was one of the youngest Corporals in The 2nd Royal Tank Regiment.*

LEFT Trevor Dady was an exceptional young soldier. He entered the Army at 15 and in 1955 he was posted to 2 RTR at Munster in Germany. Within three months he was promoted lance corporal and in less than a year he achieved corporal – one of the youngest in 2 RTR. As he said himself – 'What can possibly be better than commanding a £50,000 50-ton Centurion at the age of 20? Just incredible!' *(Photo Trevor Dady)*

barracks and in the field, which I thoroughly enjoyed. In February 1958 I was promoted to sergeant and remained as troop leader until a young officer was posted in as troop leader.

'During the time I had been in my troop we had only National Servicemen to crew the tanks. The National Servicemen usually were only trained in one tank trade before arriving in the regiment. Therefore, once a soldier had been allocated a post in a tank crew, they would remain in that post on the same tank until their demob. Every crewman would know every nut and bolt on his tank as they helped each other during maintenance periods. On occasions some National Servicemen who were more mature and showed promise to do better than others were selected to attend a promotion cadre course and possibly trained in another tank trade. Two National Servicemen in my squadron attained the rank of corporal with one also being appointed as an assistant gunnery instructor. Apart from one soldier in my troop, the others were anxious to do their time and go home. I found them to be very keen and I could not have wished for any better crewmen. One of my wireless operators came from Newcastle. He was so tall that even when standing on the fighting compartment floor, his head and shoulders were protruding out of the top of the turret. Many was the time he was told over the wireless to get down inside the turret as too much of his person was exposed.

'Sleeping arrangements for Centurion crews were very much the same throughout the regiment. We had no luxury such as sleeping bags, so we had to take our bedding blankets from barracks to sleep in. I believe some officers had canvas sleeping bags in which they would put their blankets. At the end of the day in the field, the troop leaders would be summoned

BELOW The name **BADGER** on the side stowage bins of this Centurion Mark 5 indicates that it is the tank of the squadron commander of **BADGER** Squadron 2 RTR. The tank is deeply mired in the mud and awaits recovery by the squadron ARV. Once the belly plate of the hull was in direct contact with the mud, suction was created which no amount of manoeuvring back and forth would shift, often resulting in a burnt-out clutch.

to the squadron leaders "O Group" (Orders Group) for a debriefing on the day's events and a briefing on the following day's activities. The O Groups would normally take place at dusk, so the task of getting the troop leader's bed sorted out and in position usually fell to the wireless operator while the troop leader was away at the briefing. In some troops this did not go down well with some rough National Servicemen who had National Service officers as troop leaders and did not consider themselves to be servants. Each tank was issued with a four-man bivouac, known as a "bivvy", which was tied to the side of the tank.

'The large open end was tied to the side of the tank with the sloped end of the bivvy, where the soldiers' feet would go, supported by three 18in-high poles away from the tank. Wooden pegs held the canvas sides to the ground and braced the bivvy poles. If the ground was damp, the tank turret sheet would be used as a groundsheet. When in a squadron leaguer, or encampment, the rule was for all bivvies to be erected on the inside of the leaguer. This meant that during dark hours the replenishment echelon vehicles could safely move down the other side of the line of tanks without the fear of running over men asleep in their bivvy. When in a camouflaged tactical location, or if we were to remain in the same location for some time, the tank commander would decide which side of the tank the bivvy would be erected. Usually the echelon vehicles would not be able to drive close to the tank. Therefore the possibility of being run over by an echelon vehicle was much reduced.

'On other occasions we would sleep on the engine compartment decks. The turret sheet (tarpaulin) would be passed over the depressed gun barrel and tied at the edges to the tank catwalk. The gun would then be elevated and the turret sheet would form a tent for the crew. After a day on the move, Centurion engine decks were always warm and would keep the crew cosy throughout the night. Centurion was a warm tank. Heater air could be deflected into the fighting compartment and turret from the "Aux Gen" [auxiliary generator] in the engine compartment. The main purpose of the Aux Gen was to provide electrical power for the gun control equipment. A crew who got wet could soon dry themselves, or their clothing, by

making use of the warm air deflected into the tank interior. Alternatively at the end of the day the transmission compartment decks and the radiators could be lifted and propped up, and with the engine still running, hot air could be drawn through from the engine compartment by the cooling fans, which would soon dry out and warm up the crew and their clothing.

'Meal times were normally a time when everyone on the crew got stuck in together to make the most of what the "compo" (composite) rations provided. The exception to this was usually on the troop leader's tank. The officer would take over the wireless watch while the food was prepared. Food was cooked in two ways. The first was on the little square petrol No 2 cooker that each tank had one of. The cooker came with a square Dixie cooking pot and lid. The compo rations came in a pack for five soldiers to last for two days. This, I believe, was because wartime tanks mainly had a crew of five men. As no one had bothered to update the pack suppliers, Centurion crews did well for food. It was many years later that the powers that be were made aware of the fact that tanks now had a four-man crew. Consequently rations were reduced and we would have to make sure we did not consume all the contents of the pack, but to save some

BELOW 09BA52 CAVALIER of 2 Troop, CYCLOPS Squadron, 2 RTR, was the Centurion Mark 5 of Sergeant Trevor Dady (on the right) during his service in BAOR in 1957. Here he poses with his crew Joe, Fred and George during an exercise on Sennelager Training Area. The close camaraderie and co-operation of the crew was essential for the efficient operation of any tank. In the 1950s, National Servicemen made up a significant proportion of the British Army's manpower. *(Photo Trevor Dady)*

for the next ration issue. The contents of the compo tins that had been selected for the meal would be emptied into the Dixie and heated on the cooker. When cooked, the contents would be shared between the crew. Usually this meant that most main meals were an 'all-in-stew'.

'The meals were supplemented by bread issued by the squadron SQMS (squadron quartermaster sergeant) every other day, or hard tack biscuits contained in the compo packs. Sometimes the three tank crews in the troop might combine the cooking so that they had a choice of food from the ration packs. The ten-man ration packs, with a different selection of contents, were issued on a random basis, unless you got on well with the squadron storeman. He might let you select your ration pack before others arrived to collect theirs for their tank crew. Each ration pack had a letter from the alphabet marked on its side ranging from A to H. The contents of all packs were in tins, including the tin opener that was usually within the tin of sweets. Some packs would contain tinned fruit, a variety of meat-based main meals, sausages and bacon. All packs contained chocolate, sweets, oatmeal biscuits, tea, tinned milk, sugar, matches and toilet paper. Once you got to know the contents of each pack you would do your best to get the pack most favoured for its contents for your crew at the time of issue. There were no instructions on how to cook the meals, you just learned the hard way or listened to advice from soldiers who had previous experience.

'When on exercises we would try to supplement our rations by swapping our compo with local farmers for eggs and vegetables. The Germans liked our tins of chocolate in particular, which we would swap for fresh food. On occasions when near a field of growing potatoes, and with no farmer around, we would go and dig up sufficient potatoes to last us a few days. So Centurion crews never went hungry. The lid of the Dixie could be used as a frying pan using the margarine from the ration pack to fry eggs if we had managed to obtain some. The second way of cooking your meal was by lifting the transmission compartment decks and laying tins of compo along the top of the tank radiators. When mealtimes arrived we would lift the transmission decks and retrieve the heated tins. The tins never got hot enough to make them explode. Caution had to be taken, though, when piercing the tins, as the hot contents could squirt out on the unsuspecting crew member. This method of cooking was favoured when halt parades were carried out or if it was known that time would be short before moving off again. The tin would be passed around the crew who would spoon out what they wanted into their mess tin. If time was really short the tin would be passed around, each crew member taking and eating a spoonful of the contents before passing it round until the tin was empty. Each tank crew would dig a hole in which to bury discarded tins and other rubbish before moving off. Another very important item of the tank equipment was the electric brewing vessel, or boiling vessel universally known as the "BV". The BV was a saucepan-shaped vessel containing an electric element similar to those in electric kettles of today. It could hold about half a gallon of water. In use, its electric lead had to be plugged into a socket at the bottom rear of the fighting compartment near where the wireless operator would stand. Power to heat the BV came from the Aux Gen. With the Aux Gen running, it would bring the water inside to boiling in about 4 minutes. Tea would be made in the pot and poured out into the crew's mugs. Tea being a very important beverage, it was in regular demand during exercises. During some exercises when the tanks were constantly on the move, it would be hours before a crew could have a brew. To overcome this problem

BELOW CAVALIER engages a target on the gunnery ranges at Hohne. The main armament was the Ordnance Quick Firing 20-pounder Mark 1 with a calibre of 3.3in. The Armour Piercing Discarding Sabot round had a muzzle velocity of 4,800ft/sec with the ability to penetrate a thickness of armour seven times the diameter of the core or four times the calibre of the shot at normal impact and point-blank range.
(Photo Trevor Dady)

I made a "table" for my tank out of a piece of plywood that was fitted and strapped inside the main armament deflector shield which protected the turret crew from the recoil of the main armament. When travelling with the gun stabiliser on and the "Gun Front", the brew pot could be placed on the "table" and connected to the Aux Gen power point, meaning the water for the tea boiled while we were on the move. The stabiliser would keep the brew pot table level at all times, thus avoiding spillage. The gunner would be under instruction not to traverse the turret until the tea was made and the BV disconnected from the power point. This practice could only be carried out when moving "non–tactically" or on a road march when traversing the turret was not practical, and of course whenever we were not liable to be firing any main armament or blank ammunition.

ABOVE A quartet of Centurions undertakes a 'troop shoot': these tanks have a mixture of A and B Type 20-pounder barrels. The high muzzle velocity of the 20-pounder caused significant obscuration on firing and thus made it difficult to observe the fall of shot. Obscuration is the amount of dust and debris thrown up by the gun blast on firing, which often meant that the gunner and commander could not see whether the round had hit the target.

'In the 1950s Centurion was equipped with the wireless set No 19 and a smaller wireless set No 88. Both sets were powered by 24V. The 88 set was for use when working with infantry and only had a limited range of about two miles. The HF [high-frequency] 19 set was for communications between tanks within the squadron. The 19 set contained two independent sets within the wireless itself. The "A" set was for the squadron intercommunications and the "B"

LEFT Gunnery training at Hohne was often the highlight of a tank crew's year, but the annual Administrative Inspection (AI) definitely was not. Each tank was rigorously inspected by higher command to ensure that every vehicle was ready for war. The AI entailed weeks of laborious effort as the tanks were stripped, cleaned, painted and 'bulled' until they gleamed. This is a line-up of Centurion Mark 5s of CYCLOPS Squadron, 2 RTR, on their 1956 AI at Munster. *(Photo Trevor Dady)*

set was supposed to be used for inter-tank communications within the troop. The "B" set was not used very often as it could cause confusion when trying to listen simultaneously to orders being given over the "A" set. The "B" set aerial was a short screw-in rod, about 2ft long, which fitted into a vertical rubber aerial base on the top of the turret. It was positioned a distance from the "A" set aerial so as not to cause electrical interference between the two wireless set aerials. The main "A" set had a range of about 12 miles, but was notorious for going "'off net" [off frequency] and was a headache for the wireless operator who would constantly have to check the tuning of his set. The tuning signal would be transmitted by the squadron signals sergeant from whichever vehicle the squadron leader was commanding the squadron at the time. As the 19 set was an HF set, aerial rods could be erected in 4ft sections up to 12ft to gain better reception and transmissions and by electronically tuning the aerial with the wireless variometer. Normally 8ft of aerial on the tank would suffice. Communications within the tank were effected by voice signals passing through the wireless set and controlled by various switches on grey control boxes fitted inside the tank, where each crew member would plug in his personal headset. The tank commander also had a "Tannoy handset", which gave him direct contact with the driver only. In the early 1960s the 19 set was replaced by the more up-to-date HF Cl2 radio.

'At the rear of the tank was the infantry tank telephone contained within an armoured box with a hinged access lid. The purpose of the tank telephone was for supporting infantry to talk to the tank commander whenever he was requesting supporting tank gunfire. To attract the attention of the tank commander, the infantryman would have to get to the rear of the tank, open the access lid and press a button that would sound a buzzer in the commander's headphones. The infantryman would then press a pressel switch and talk to the tank commander. With all the noise going on in the tank and outside, it was sometimes difficult to attract the tank commander's attention by the telephone. Many an infantryman has had to jump away rapidly when the tank moved off, or worse reversed, while he was attempting to use the phone, with the commander unaware of the presence of the infantryman. Many a joke has been played on infantrymen when working closely together and in a non-tactical position. A tank crewman would go to the tank telephone and pull out the handset, and then in full view of the infantry, would have a pretend long conversation with someone. The call would end with the tankman saying: "I will give you a call next week Mum." The infantrymen would fall for this joke every time as the tankman had given the impression that he had been able to telephone his mother in England from the tank telephone in Germany.

'Because of the limited range of early Centurions, each tank was issued with a Mono-trailer containing 200 gallons of petrol, which was towed behind the tank. The Mono-trailer was hitched to the rear of the tank by two arms, which hooked up to quick-release hooks on the tank. The Mono-trailer was lifted into position by the use of two hand-operated "Tirfor" ratchet winches provided by the squadron fitters. The Mono-trailer could also be secured by the hooks but suspended with the wheel off the ground by chains so that the Centurion with Mono-trailer attached could be loaded on to a tank transporter.

'The idea behind the Mono-trailer was that the petrol it contained would be used on the approach march to the battlefield start line. It would then be jettisoned, leaving the tank to move forward using fuel contained in the engine compartment fuel tanks. When needed on the approach march, the fuel from the Mono-trailer would be pumped into the tank's internal fuel tanks through a connecting fuel pipe by means of the tank bilge pump. Problems encountered with the towed Mono-trailer could be quite startling. When drawing from the Mono-trailer on the march, the driver would have to monitor the fuel gauges very carefully. When the fuel in the internal fuel tanks dropped to a low level, he would switch on the tank bilge pump, which would transfer fuel from the Mono-trailer into the Centurion's fuel tanks. If the driver became distracted and did not watch the fuel gauges, the fuel being transferred from the Mono-trailer could overflow into the engine compartment. This situation was always very alarming as the spilt petrol could easily catch light in the hot engine compartment, with disastrous results. When the Mono-trailer was safely hooked up to the rear of the tank, a small explosive charge in the form of an FE 103 (fuse electric 103) was fitted into a recess in the Mono-trailer hooks at the rear of the tank. Once the FE 103 was connected, the Mono-trailer could be released from the tank by pressing a button in the tank, which exploded the FE 103. This disengaged the hooks and allowed the Mono-trailer to drop away. A self-sealing fuel pipe connector prevented fuel escaping from the trailer.

'Moving cross-country, occasionally a Mono-trailer arm would disengage from the hook on the tank and drop to the ground. This was a situation that all tank commanders feared. When one arm fell away, it meant that the other arm was being twisted as it tried to take the full weight of the Mono-trailer and the remaining fuel. The fuel pipe from the trailer to the tank was attached to the right-hand Mono-trailer arm. If the right-hand arm fell away there was the possibility that the fuel pipe may be damaged allowing fuel to escape – although, the fuel pipe was fitted with a self-sealing connector, which would hopefully prevent fuel escaping. The commander and wireless operator had to continually look to the rear of the tank to see that the Mono-trailer was behaving as it should, and had not become detached in any way. The Mono-trailer wheel had the ability to rotate 360 degrees and would turn 180 degrees whenever the tank reversed. Reversing Centurion with a Mono-trailer attached over rough ground could end in disaster. If the commander allowed

the Mono-trailer wheel to drop into a hole or ditch, the tank would sometimes reverse over the trailer, usually breaking or bending the trailer arms beyond repair. A Mono-trailer still containing petrol in this situation certainly posed recovery problems. When in barracks most Mono-trailers were usually detached and parked at the rear of the tank hangar. On the top of the Mono-trailer was a 2ft circular access plate held down with about 18 bolts. On return to barracks from an exercise, one of the troop Mono-trailers would have the access plate removed, thereby giving the troop access to petrol for cleaning tools and other equipment. On reflection years later, this was very wasteful and dangerous. But petrol was not in short supply to us then. Like all military vehicles each Mono-trailer had its own registration number and often its own name. It had to be inspected for serviceability and faults each month.

'All maintenance on Centurion had to be routinely recorded. Each day the driver would have to complete a record of vehicle mileage and hours run by the tank engine and the Aux Gen. He also had to record how much oil and fuel had been used and what servicing had been carried out. This was recorded in the AB 413 [Army Book 413, known by the crews as the 413]. This task was never very accurate and was quite a headache for the drivers who could only guess what figures should be entered in the 413. Any crew member could start the main engine or Aux Gen during the day while carrying out servicing tasks, or even making a brew. The driver may be away from the tank on

ABOVE The failure of the 200-gallon Mono-trailer prompted the design of an alternative supplementary fuel tank for the Centurion gun tank. The result was an armoured 100-gallon tank bolted to the rear hull plate, which increased the vehicle length but effectively doubled its range, and made it far less prone to damage across country or in road traffic accidents.

ABOVE In 1953–54 the Royal Netherlands Army received 592 Centurions under the Mutual Defense Assistance Program whereby the USA provided much of the finance to re-equip NATO armies during the Cold War. The tanks were fitted with American radio sets and Browning coaxial machine guns to make them Centurion Mark 5s. They were progressively modernised over the years with L7 105mm guns, IR equipment and ranging guns.

other duties and would therefore have no idea of what fuel the tank may have used. The daily entry in the 413 was supposed to be agreed by the tank commander. Actually reconciling the hours run and fuel used usually fell to the troop sergeant, who would take the troop 413s to a quiet spot and spend an hour or two trying to "balance the books" each week. This was mainly an awful lot of guesswork and manipulating figures to try to make things look right. Each 413 was supposed to be signed off by the troop leader each week as a true record! Troop leaders usually did as they were told by the troop sergeant, so would sign off the 413s. In most cases no one senior to the troop leader would inspect or look at the 413s, which was a good thing as far as we were concerned. Petrol used for cleaning tools and equipment from the Mono-trailers was usually accounted for by declaring it had become "contaminated". This meant it could no longer be transferred to the Centurion's fuel tanks. As there was no procedure for disposing of "contaminated" fuel we could dispose of it as we wished.

'Each month every vehicle was required to undergo an inspection to locate any mechanical and electrical faults. The reason for the inspection was to find out whether the crew were operating the tank and equipment correctly and carrying out routine servicing as laid down. The inspection would also provide the commanding officer and squadron leaders with an accurate picture of the state of readiness of vehicles. This inspection would be carried out by the troop leader or by any one of the troop NCOs. The inspection was carried out using a large checklist on an "Inspection Form AFG 857", known to crews as "the 857". The 857 inspection covered every mechanical and electrical item of equipment on the tank. The person carrying out the 857 would list his findings as an "A" job, "B" job or a "C" job. An "A" job was a fault that was to be corrected by a crew member, such as missing nuts and bolts or servicing overdue. A "B" job was a task that required the attention of a squadron fitter. A "C" job was a major task that would normally be carried out by a base workshop and not within the regiment. Applying a "C" job status was usually the decision of the officer in charge of the LAD (regimental light aid detachment). This officer, usually with the rank of captain, was known as the EME (electrical and mechanical engineer). The completed 857 would be copied to the squadron fitter staff sergeant for action where required and to the squadron leader for information as to the state of the squadron tanks. The original sheet of the 857 would be kept in the troop with the tank documents. The crew members who were responsible for correcting the "A" jobs would be tasked accordingly.

'One monthly task that had to be carried out was that of testing the main armament recoil system. Annual firing was the only time when absolutely everything on the tank was operated

LEFT With a red flag flying to denote live firing is in progress, a Centurion Mark 3 or 5 fires on the gunnery ranges with an instructor observing from the turret rear. The Ordnance Quick Firing 20-pounder Mark 1 as fitted to Centurion Marks 3 and 5 was a supremely accurate weapon and with the introduction of APDS Mark 3 and 4 rounds it had few equals in the world in the 1950s as to penetration performance against opposing armour.

at the same time. To check the recoil system during the 857 inspection when in barracks, the gun was "pulled back". This involved inserting a pulley wheel into the end of the barrel, passing a steel cable from a turret lifting eye round the pulley wheel and back to another lifting eye to which a hand Tirfor ratchet winch had been attached. The procedure was to winch the gun back to its maximum recoil position, while a crew member would check the recoil cylinders inside the turret for leaks. If everything was satisfactory, the quick-release catch on the Tirfor winch would be struck with a hammer, allowing the gun to go forward under pressure from the recoil system. Prior to moving to the ranges for annual firing the squadron gunfitter would check the bore of the barrel to gauge the wear.

'In Germany, Centurions in the 1950s and 1960s were limited to a total mileage of about 3,000 before being sent back to base workshops for a complete overhaul. Therefore all movement to the training areas was either by tank transporter or by rail. Loading Centurion on to the low-loader pulled by a Diamond T tractor transporter unit was quite a daunting experience for the novice driver. The tank would be lined up to the transporter trailer and then guided on by a crew member standing on the front of the trailer where he could be seen by the driver. There was very little room for error as the tank would eventually have to be lashed down with an equal couple of inches of track overhanging each side – exactly the length of a box of Swan Vestas. As the tank climbed up on to the trailer, the driver would lose sight of everything and would only be able to see the sky until the tank slowly moved forward beyond the fulcrum point and dropped down on to the trailer when the person guiding him could be seen again. Some nervous drivers would commit the sin of accelerating when all they could see was the sky. The tank would go forward rather rapidly as if out of control. Many a guiding person has had to leap off the trailer to get out of the way. However, loading and unloading came with practice.

'At one time in Germany the authorities decided that the combined weight of the tank transporter and Centurion was too great for some bridges. The tanks would have to be unloaded at each bridge and the transporter driven across followed by the tank. The tank

would then have to be reloaded and lashed down again which was rather a long-winded task. Because of these restrictions, I can recall one occasion where a journey by car that would have taken 4 hours to the training area, took the transporter convoy the best part of a week. Once he was satisfied with the position of the tank, two railway sleepers had to be carried from a wagon at the front of the train to the flat and laid under the tank tracks at the front and rear of the tank to prevent any forward or rearward movement. The tank had also to be lashed down with chains and shackles. Feeding on the train was sometimes by crews using their No 2 petrol cookers or an issue of sandwiches and tea.

'The highlight of the training year was annual firing on Hohne Ranges. However, we were limited to the number of main armament rounds that could be fired as only the qualified gunners had this privilege. Each gunner had to qualify in all range practices firing AP, HE, smoke and canister rounds, as well as firing practices with the coaxial machine gun. At the end of each firing day the wear on each barrel had to be assessed. The actual wear was calculated by a system known as EFCs (equivalent full charge). A 20-pounder gun barrel was only supposed to fire a total of 60 EFCs before it was worn out and had to be changed for a new one. For example, the value of an APDS round was 0.5 of an EFC. HE rounds had a far lower EFC value of just 0.05. Smoke rounds had such a negligible EFC value that it was usually ignored.

'When firing the various combined practices the best way of checking the EFC values of rounds fired was to stand the spent shell cases beside the tank in groups of APDS, HE and

ABOVE **The Centurions of 3 Troop CYCLOPS Squadron of 2 RTR manoeuvre during troop training with the troop leader's 05ZR47 COUGAR to the fore. The annual training cycle remained fairly standard over the Cold War years with personal training prevalent during the winter months followed by training as a troop during the early spring with progressively as a squadron then regiment until the major formation exercises in the autumn following the harvest when the tanks would do least damage to agricultural land.**

smoke, etc. The types of rounds the gun had fired could then be determined and the EFC value arrived at. The troop leader would usually be called upon to record the EFC wear of the guns being fired in his troop, and when nearing the 60 EFC point would call in the squadron gunfitter to check the bore for wear. Before any live main armament firing could begin, the sight gear would have to be tested and adjusted and the gun "bore sighted". This meant checking that the gunner's sight and the centre of the bore of the main armament were pointing at exactly the same point at 1,000yd. Early methods of bore sighting involved placing two pieces of thread across the end of the barrel, held in place in grooves on the end of the barrel by grease. The firing needle assembly then had to be removed from the breechblock. The commander, or gunnery instructor, using one eyepiece of a pair of binoculars, would instruct the gunner to traverse or elevate the gun until the cross-threads on the end of the barrel were on the centre of the target at 1,000yd. The gunner's sight would then be adjusted using the periscope graticule-adjusting knobs to move the graticule pattern to the same point on the target. Later a "muzzle bore sight" was brought into service, which did away with the need to use the cross-threads and binoculars.

'Before firing, the gun barrel would be scrubbed and cleaned by the crew using the bore brush on the end of the six cleaning rods (officially named "staves intermediate"). After cleaning, to prevent dirt entering the gun barrel, a piece of cloth or cotton waste would be plugged into the end of the barrel. On occasions the crew would forget the rag or waste was still in the barrel and commence firing – with disastrous results if the first round was HE. On leaving the barrel the round would explode. This was known as a "premature". After a premature, firing from all tanks would be suspended and an immediate inquiry held to ascertain the cause. The fear was that the ammunition batch was suspect. This had to be ruled out and a satisfactory conclusion had to be reached before firing could recommence. If the ammunition was suspected of being faulty, it would be withdrawn and would then be inspected by the Royal Army Ordnance Corps ammunition technician. Usually it was found to be a fault of a crew member not removing the obstruction prior to firing. A crew that had caused the premature by leaving the rag or cotton waste in the barrel would not be very popular, as it meant main armament firing was delayed. The crew would most certainly receive a dressing-down by the squadron leader and gunnery instructors. Later, similar cases of a premature were caused by the muzzle bore sight being left in the end of the barrel after the testing and adjusting of the gun and sight gear. As well as the obligatory dressing-down, the person responsible for leaving the bore sight in the gun would have to pay for a replacement, which was quite expensive. As a result of prematures being caused by crews, a drill was introduced where before firing the first round, or after a long delay in firing, the loader would have to open the breech, peer down the barrel and report to the commander "bore clear" – or "bore foul" if he could see an obstruction.

'Checking for ground clearance was part of the HE drill when firing from a hull-down or turret-down position to ensure that the round would not strike the ground forward of the tank. Having established a strike on the target when firing HE, sometimes the commander would wish to put down a few more rounds quickly to completely destroy the target area. This was known as "fire for effect". As the muzzle velocity of HE was 2,000ft per second, the trajectory out to the maximum range of 8,900yd was quite a high "lob". At a range of 2,000yd or more, the crew would often try to get three

BELOW **COBRA and COUGAR of 3 Troop CYCLOPS Squadron await their turn on the gunnery ranges. These tanks have sheet metal auxiliary fuel tanks as fabricated in REME Workshops in West Germany that were widely used before the advent of the Mono-trailer. Displayed on the back, from left to right, is the insignia of 6th Armoured Division, the vehicle call-sign Six Three Bravo and the arm of service sign with the number 51 superimposed to denote 2 RTR as the senior armoured regiment within the division.** *(Photo Trevor Dady)*

HE rounds in the air at one time, sometimes in competition with another tank if conducting a troop shoot on the same target area. The procedure for getting three rounds in the air was not an official drill or practice. The way this was done was that on receiving the order "fire for effect" from the commander, the loader would load one round into the breech, select and hold another round between his knees, then pick up and cradle another round in his arms.

'Firing on Centurion was on an electrical system. The gunner would hold the electrical firing switch down during this practice. When ready, the loader would flick the loader's safety switch to "fire", which completed the firing circuit and thus the gun would fire. On the gun moving forward after recoil and automatically ejecting the spent shell case, the loader would load the second round, then pick up and cradle the third round in his arms, then again flick the loader's safety switch to "fire". The gun would again fire. The loader would then load the third round and again fire it from the loader's safety switch. This practice needed very swift and careful actions from the loader. On one occasion I remember a loader did not ensure the next round to be fired, which was in his arms, was outside the tubular gun deflector. The projectile of this round was in fact inside the deflector and was struck by the breech block on recoil. The loader also had not obeyed the instruction to never hold the base of the round in the spread-out palm of the right hand. Consequently, on recoil, the breech struck this round, pushing it to the rear. The loader's hand holding the base of the round was thrust back on to the front of the wireless set No 19. His hand and wrist bones were broken as they made rapid contact with the front of the 19 set.

'APDS rounds were for engaging enemy armoured vehicles. Firing APDS was always looked forward to by the crews as the muzzle velocity was 4,700ft per second and had spectacular effects when striking a hard target. On the ranges a hard target was usually a derelict tank hull or some armoured plate placed on the range to represent enemy armour. The maximum range for engaging hard targets was 3,000yd. Until the advent of ranging guns fitted to Centurion, most firing practices used the target bracketing method until a strike was achieved. A round failing to go off when the firing switch sequence was completed was known as a "misfire". Causes of misfires were usually due to slow-burning cordite within the shell case. The misfire drill was always followed to the letter, which meant several checks to ensure all the electrical switching of the firing circuit was correct. If no faults were found, the order "wait 30 minutes" was given by the commander. Ordnance tests had proved that after 30 minutes it was very unlikely that the round would go off. At the end of the 30-minute wait, the round would be unloaded by the loader and carefully passed out of the turret to someone nominated who would then lower the round to someone on the ground. That person would then take the round to a point at the end of the firing point where it would remain until disposed of by a member of the range staff or an ammunition technician from the Ordnance Corps. The persons involved in the removal of the "misfire" to the safe area at the end of the range usually needed a cup of tea after this hair-raising experience.

'One occasion I will never forget was when as the gunnery instructor I was coaching a certain rather hot-headed second lieutenant troop leader through an HE shoot when he had a "misfire". We went through the misfire drill, as laid down, and then I ordered "wait 30 minutes". I noted the time and we waited. 25 minutes later the troop leader ordered the loader to unload the round. I shouted "Stop!" to the loader. The

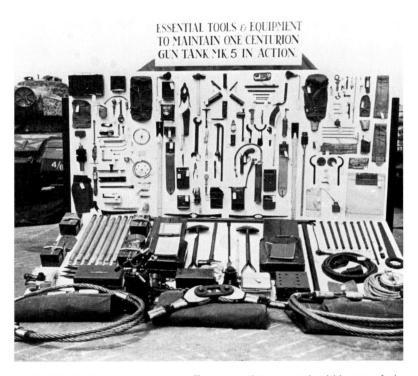

ESSENTIAL TOOLS & EQUIPMENT TO MAINTAIN ONE CENTURION GUN TANK MK 5 IN ACTION.

ABOVE All the tools that were needed, to keep a tank running in the field – basic and specialised – were known as the Complete Equipment Schedule and were carried on the tank. Even though the Centurion was adequately provided with stowage bins, there was never enough room for all the personal kit that a crew wished to take on exercise as well. This excluded, of course, a full load of ammunition and combat rations.

young officer turned to me and said he was fed up waiting and wanted the round unloaded. We got into an argument but as the IG [instructor of gunnery] I had the last word. Then, at exactly the 29-minute point, the round went off. Had the round been out of the chamber it would have had disastrous results. I duly received an apology from the young officer concerned.

'Coaxial machine gun firing with .30-cal Browning was also part of the annual range firing. It took a lot of persuading to get the gunner to use short bursts and watch the fall of shot before giving longer bursts. Most gunners would try to hosepipe the fall of shot to the target with very long, wasteful bursts. The barrel life of the .30-cal Browning was only 11 belts of ammunition before it was shot out and would have to be replaced. The .30-cal ammunition came in steel boxes of 250 cloth-belted rounds. Each belt would contain rounds in the order of four ball, followed by one red-tipped tracer round to aid observation.

'Firing the multi-barrelled smoke grenade dischargers was always looked forward to. The result of the firing was always a spectacular display that never failed to fill spectators with awe. The smoke grenade dischargers were, for safety's sake, always loaded from behind the discharger. First an FE 103 would be placed

in the discharger barrel with the connecting leads passed through a hole in the base of the barrel and connected to an electrical terminal block. The electrical circuit would be checked to ensure there were no short circuits. Next the WP [White Phosphorous] No 80 grenade would be inserted into the barrel. The safety ring and pin would be pulled out just prior to the time for firing the discharger. On pressing a button inside the turret, the FE 103 would explode and project the grenades about 50yd forward of the tank where they would explode forming a screen of white smoke. The smoke grenade discharger had a series of six barrels on each side of the turret facing forward. The barrels were set at an angle so as to spread the grenades when fired to form a smokescreen. The commander could determine how many barrels, in multiples of two, he wished to fire.

'A small fuse was ignited when the grenade left the barrel and the sprung lever released. A few seconds later, a small explosive in the grenade detonated, which burst the grenade canister. White Phosphorous ignited on contact with air and formed a dense cloud of white smoke. Whenever White Phosphorous grenades were being handled and fired, buckets of water were placed near the tank for safety. In the event of anyone being contaminated by White Phosphorous, the burning part of the body or clothing would have to be immediately immersed in water to put it out. Copper oxide paste was held by medical staff so that in the event of a phosphorous burn on any part of the body, it could be applied to stop air getting to the phosphorous, thus preventing the burning from continuing. The person sustaining the burn would need immediate medical treatment.

'Simulation of main armament gunfire in the 1950s was very limited. If we were very lucky we would be issued with a few blank rounds for our Centurion 20-pounder while on exercise. It was up to the tank commander to use his discretion during exercises as to when these prized blanks were to be fired, to give the best impression to the "enemy" or to umpires. In addition to the main armament blanks, commanders were issued with a few Verey cartridges to fire from their "pistol signals", to represent main armament fire. Thunder flashes were also issued to supplement the former methods of gunfire. These methods of representing gunfire, apart from firing blanks, tended to leave a little to be desired. Then came the Hohne Organ.

'The Hohne Organ, as we knew it, comprised of two semi-circular clamps, or brackets, with four tubes welded to each clamp. Each tube was about 8in long and 2in in diameter. The front end of the tube was slightly flared and the rear end was blanked off with a hole of about 0.25in diameter centrally drilled through. The two parts of the clamp would be bolted together around the 20-pounder A-type barrel counterweight sleeve. To ensure a good electrical earth, paint would be scraped off the metal where the clamp made contact with the counterweight sleeve.

'Each tank was issued with a number of "bags puff powder", which were small bags of a cotton-type of material, filled with a minor explosive powder. A corresponding number of small electrical two-wire detonators would also be issued. To arm the Hohne Organ, a bag puff powder was pierced and a detonator inserted into the powder. The bag and detonator would then be pushed into the Hohne Organ tube with the electrical wires passing through the hole at the back of the tube. One of the detonator wires would be wrapped around one of the bolts clamping the organ to the gun barrel to provide an electrical earth. The other wire was connected to a length of Don 8 wire, snipped from the turrets mounted "reels cable", and taped along the gun barrel. The other end of the Don 8 was connected to a smoke discharger terminal on the outside of the turret. This procedure was repeated, connecting to different smoke discharger terminals, until all eight Hohne Organ tubes had been "loaded". When wishing to simulate gunfire, the commander would simply press one of the smoke discharger buttons inside the turret, then the detonator would be activated electrically, thus detonating the bag puff powder, which gave an impressive puff of smoke to resemble main armament firing. After eight firings, the loading procedure would be repeated.

'Enthusiasm really went to our heads on many occasions when reloading. Instead of only one bag puff powder being inserted into the tube, sometimes as many as three would

be forced in, which gave a more impressive puff of smoke. Unofficially, to add to the bang of the detonator and bag puff powder, sometimes a FE 103 (for discharging the White Phosphorous 80 grenade from the smoke dischargers) would be inserted instead of the regulation detonator, with quite impressive and sometimes alarming results. As a wireless operator on our troop leader's tank in 1956, I can remember we reloaded our Hohne Organ with more than the recommended number of bags puff powder. The exercise was going very well and the Hohne Organ was giving very impressive simulated gunfire. Our commander, having fired one of the tubes, heard a whirring sound as something passed his left ear, and asked, "What was that?" Next time we reloaded our Hohne Organ, we were only able to load seven of the tubes, as we discovered that the additional bags puff powder we had earlier loaded had blown out the rear of one of the tubes. The whirring sound earlier heard by our commander was the back end of the tube passing his head!

'Hohne Organs could only be fitted to Centurions with A-type barrels. The later B-type barrels had a fume extractor halfway down the barrel, and no counterweight and sleeve at the forward end to take the organ. Once again, compared to today's methods of simulating gunfire and electronically disabling "enemy" tanks on exercises, our gunfire simulation was really of the Stone Age, but it was better than nothing and great fun. As of course was Centurion.'

Chapter Six

Centurion in combat

With such a diverse combat record, it is fitting that the actions of Centurion in British Army service should begin in Korea, when it fired its first round in action on 11 February 1951 and conclude with its final campaign during the Gulf War of 1991.

OPPOSITE The Centurion first saw combat during the Korean War of 1950 to 1953. However, the mountainous terrain was totally unsuited to the employment of heavy armour and at 50 tons Centurion was the heaviest tank in theatre. Here, COTTAGE II of 3 Troop, C Squadron, 8th King's Royal Irish Hussars demonstrates its hill-climbing ability from where devastating direct fire could be brought to bear on enemy positions.

Korea

The grand alliance between the Western Powers and the Soviet Union soon dissipated into acrimony after the victory parades of 1945 that marked the defeat of Nazi Germany and its Axis partners. When Josef Stalin imposed Communist governments in those Eastern European countries occupied by the Red Army, the West created the Federal Republic of Germany in June 1948, whereupon the Russians imposed a blockade on the city of Berlin that was divided between the four erstwhile Allied powers – France, Great Britain, the Soviet Union and the United States of America. The Cold War was now a reality, with the opposing forces deployed along the Inner German Border at a time of increasing pressure. The Berlin Blockade lasted for 318 days before Stalin abandoned the siege on 12 May 1949 but tension remained high. During the previous month, a military alliance of 12 Western powers was created as the North Atlantic Treaty Organization, or NATO. In response, the Soviet Union subsequently formed the Warsaw Pact, incorporating all the occupied countries of Eastern Europe. The stage was set for many years of confrontation and hostility. And the first encounter came in the far peninsula of Korea.

Under the auspices of the United Nations, a multinational army was assembled following the invasion in June 1950 of the Republic of Korea by the North Korean People's Army at the instigation of Josef Stalin. The British committed the 27th Infantry Brigade to South Korea from their station in Hong Kong, soon followed by 29th Independent Infantry Brigade Group. The latter was supported by the Centurion tanks of the 8th Kings Royal Irish Hussars and together they trained north from the port of Pusan to the North Korean capital of Pyongyang where they unloaded just as the Chinese People's Volunteer Army entered the war. There ensued what was known as the 'Great Bug Out' when UN Forces fell back in disarray. The two British brigades retreated as well, but at no time were the tanks in contact with the enemy. In sub-zero temperatures and on frozen unmetalled roads, the brand-new Centurion tanks, some with just 28 miles on their clocks, were pushed to the limits as they withdrew some 200 miles to Suwon where they spent Christmas. Despite the appalling conditions, the Centurions performed admirably without breakdowns – although one had to be abandoned to the enemy when it shed its tracks and there were no recovery vehicles to tow it to safety.

During the bitter winter of 1950/51 with temperatures dropping to -45°F, the British awaited the inevitable Chinese offensive. As one subaltern observed on 9 January 1951: 'This has been one of the bloodiest days I can remember . . . we have given up thinking about the Chinese . . . all we could do is throw snowballs at them . . . did a 2½ hour stag at 4am in a state of numbness and semi-consciousness'. Five days before, the Battle of Happy Valley had seen the Cromwell tanks of the recce troop, 8th Hussars, and the Cromwell AOPs of 45 Field Regiment RA, fighting in support of the Royal Ulster Rifles while C Squadron, 7RTR, supported the Royal Northumberland Fusiliers. Casualties in men and machines were high.

With the coming of spring, the UN Forces began a series of concerted attacks that forced the enemy back to the 38th Parallel, the erstwhile international border between North and South Korea. On 22 April 1951, the Chinese Communist Forces and North Korean People's Army launched their Spring Offensive. The full weight of the assault fell upon the two British Commonwealth brigades on the Imjin River and at Kapyong. Against

BELOW The winter of 1950/51 was bitterly cold even by Korean standards but the Centurions of the 8th King's Royal Irish Hussars performed admirably in the sub-zero conditions during the retreat from Pyongyang in December 1950. Although brand new, the Centurions withdrew almost 300 miles without mechanical mishap before making a stand on the Han River in Seoul. Here, 01ZR46 COLOMBO of 3 Troop C Squadron with Lieutenant Mickey Radford in command manoeuvres on an icy Seoul Island on 20 December 1950.

the most fearful odds, the enemy was held long enough for further defence lines to be established as the Communists crashed against the British (and Commonwealth) hilltop infantry positions in repeated human waves never experienced before by the British Army – even in Burma. Fighting on widely separated hills, the 1st Battalion Gloucestershire Regiment, 1st Battalion Royal Northumberland Fusiliers and 1st Battalion Royal Ulster Rifles fought against impossible odds of over 15 to 1. Nevertheless, British infantrymen in defence have few equals and they exacted a staggering level of casualties on the enemy before withdrawing after three exhausting days and nights under the covering guns of the artillery and the Centurions of the 8th Hussars on 25 April.

The corps commander arrived at 29 Brigade HQ at 1000 hours that morning and informed Brigadier Brodie that an attempt by the 65th Regimental Combat Team to relieve the Glosters had failed. This left the HQ open to attack, as the Belgian battalion protecting the position was now heavily outnumbered. At 1030 hours the brigade was ordered to withdraw as the enemy pressure was too great. Ammunition and water were running low and radio batteries exhausted.

The Northumberland Fusiliers started to withdraw under the covering fire of the tanks and escaped without further casualties. The first company of Ulsters also moved out without difficulty. The enemy threat from the north-west on the dominant feature of Kamak-San was very real and the road was under heavy and accurate mortar fire. The remainder of the Ulsters struck out south-east over the hills and so avoided the area of the pass. No 1 Troop was now at the pass with the troop leader's Centurion perched like a chamois atop a small hill, lashing out at the enemy who were building up in the southern re-entrant to the west of the road. This was the critical hour. A wave of Chinese swept down from the hills all along the west of the valley, forcing the tank commanders to close down. Lieutenant Radford (of 3 Troop) to the north, reported that the enemy was all over the valley floor. There was a very real danger that all the tanks would be trapped within this teeming cauldron. The Centurions ran the gauntlet of the treacherous ground. Sergeant Reekie's 'THREE ABLE'

was incapacitated by a smoke grenade and Sergeant Holberton's 'Four Baker' was disabled when, in an attempt to evade Chinese anti-tank teams, it careered over a steep dyke, spiking its gun in the ground.

Meanwhile, 1 Troop was struggling to keep the pass open, ably supported by about 30 sappers and the Ulsters' reserve company. As the last exhausted infantry trudged through the pass, 1 Troop pulled out, bringing some of the Ulsters with them as well as the sapper escort. At this time the hard-pressed Belgians were ordered to withdraw under the covering fire of 2 Troop, which had given them excellent support all morning. As they pulled out with the Centurions firing over the rear decks at the advancing enemy, 'TWO ABLE' stuck in reverse gear, crawling backwards at less than walking pace. When told of this Major Henry Huth, the squadron commander, gave permission for it to be destroyed, but the Belgian colonel refused. The rate of withdrawal slowed to keep station with the lame tank, which eventually reached the night-leaguer area where the Centurions came under Major Huth's direct control.

At the same time, 'Ormrodforce' had fought its way along the last lap of the valley through masses of Chinese, as 2,000 or more swarmed down from the west in an attempt to cut them off. The Centurions surged on, crushing enemy soldiers under their tracks. Sergeant Cadman in 'TWO SIX ABLE', an RHQ tank, hearing a Chinese soldier battering on his cupola hatch,

ABOVE On 11 February 1951, CAUGHOO and COLORADO of C Squadron of the 8th Hussars fired the first rounds in anger from a Centurion tank in support of an American infantry patrol along the north bank of the Han River. CAUGHOO, a Centurion Mark 3 commanded by Captain George Strachan MC begins the action by firing on a Cromwell tank captured in an earlier battle. Hidden below the bridge of a railway embankment, the Cromwell was destroyed at a range of over 3,700yd.

directed his Centurion through the wall of a building to brush him off and then ran over a machine-gun emplacement beside the road. Suddenly three platoons of enemy rose up out of a riverbed in parade ground order, only to be blown to oblivion by some of the last 20-pounder rounds. Some tanks took to the paddy fields. Few of the infantry clinging on to the rear decks survived this death ride. The tanks finally debouched from the valley and limped into the squadron leaguer area: 'the Centurions piled high with dead and wounded . . . blood ran down the sides turning the dust into crimson mud'.

Major Huth ordered 'Ormrodforce' to pass straight through to seek help for the wounded while he organised the withdrawal of the remainder of C Squadron. In an effort to speed the evacuation of 2 Troop's lame 'ABLE', Lieutenant Paul took it under tow. While the tow-line was being attached, Chinese machine-gun fire from the hills some 50yd away struck an 88 White Phosphorous grenade in the smoke discharger cups of the troop leader's tank, 'CHAUCER' (all the Centurions of the 8th Hussars were named after famous racehorses and steeplechasers). As the turret was traversed at the time, burning phosphorous flowed through the engine louvres, setting the engine on fire. With the Chinese only 30yd away, the crews baled out under covering fire from Major Huth. He then fired an AP round through each tank and quickly traversed his turret left to engage the fast-approaching

enemy. For 3 deliberate minutes the turret of 'CAMERONIAN' swung this way and that, firing long bursts of Besa into the Chinese. Only when it was absolutely necessary did Major Huth order his driver to retire. Some 100yd further back he was joined by Lieutenant John Lidsey on the other RHQ tank and together they continued the delaying action until there was an acceptable distance between the retreating infantry and the enemy. The two tanks then pulled back rapidly half a mile down the road to a new crisis.

Exhausted and wounded Ulsters were struggling towards the road from the hills to the east. Ordering those tanks which had halted in the vicinity to load to capacity with the infantry and withdraw, Major Huth and Lieutenant Lidsey moved forward again in an attempt to push the enemy back. For almost an hour the two Centurions fought a brilliant and courageous rearguard action. Each time the Chinese infantry were about to outflank the point tank, it withdrew some 200yd under the covering fire of the other. The Chinese followed the tanks in hordes at distances frequently less than 50yd, quite oblivious to their casualties. In Major Huth's words: 'We must have killed hundreds', but he measured his firepower against the speed of the approaching enemy so accurately that he imposed the minimum rate of advance upon them, allowing the infantry precious minutes to gain safety. Two other tanks eventually arrived to strengthen the rearguard, but not until the last infantryman was seen to reach the MSR (main supply route) where more potent firepower was available to them, did Major Huth give the order to withdraw. The last shot fired by Major Huth ended the Battle of the Imjin River.

Only the Glosters had not withdrawn. At dawn on the 25th, the Glosters with their dead and wounded about them were still on Hill 235. The guns of 45 Field Regiment had given them protection all night and before sunrise Col Carne told the drum-major to blow a long reveille. Roland's horn among the mountains, gathering echoes from centuries of battle, sounded again and the haggard soldiers on their blackened hilltop rose and cheered. Then the assault came in again. . . .

That night the Glosters received permission to break out, but, totally encircled by thousands of Chinese, few were able to do so and those remaining were captured. The brigade had lost a quarter of its strength, but had it not been for the Centurions of the 8th Hussars it is unlikely that the Belgians, Fusiliers or Ulsters could have been saved at all.

The next battle of note was Operation Commando in October 1951 when the 1st Commonwealth Division staged an offensive to gain a series of hills to provide a coherent defensive line before the approaching winter. Its success was greatly enhanced by the extraordinary mobility and fire support of the Centurion tanks that climbed seemingly unscalable heights to bring direct fire to bear on the enemy as the infantry assaults went in with 20-pounder fire some 50yd in front of the infantry and Besa coaxial at 20yd keeping the Chinese in cover until the last moment. Once these hills were captured they remained the front line for the Commonwealth Division for the next two years while peace talks continued acrimoniously at Panmunjom. And it was on these very hills that the Centurions of the 5th Royal Inniskilling Dragoon Guards and 1st Royal Tank Regiment fought a curious war for armour as static pillboxes providing intimate direct fire support to the infantry by day and night.

On 7 December 1952, the 1st Royal Tank Regiment landed at the port of Pusan in South Korea, by which time the front lines had become static with the opposing sides deeply entrenched on the commanding heights across the breadth of the Korean peninsula. 1 RTR was to replace the 5th Royal Inniskilling Dragoon Guards as the armoured regiment attached to 1st Commonwealth Division that formed part of the United Nations forces containing Communist aggression in the far-distant country of Korea. By 0700 hours on 9 December, the takeover was complete and the '5th Skins' departed for the Middle East. 1 RTR was at war for the first time since 1945.

The role of the tanks was to provide direct fire support by day and night to the infantry companies entrenched along the front lines. On the 1st British Commonwealth Division frontage, these positions were on hilltops overlooking a wide valley with the enemy similarly entrenched

ABOVE Following Operation Commando, the front line became static with the opposing armies occupying the commanding features across the breadth of the Korean peninsula. The tanks were emplaced on hilltops with their suspension and tracks protected by earthworks and sandbags. Here, a Centurion Mark 3 of the 5th Royal Inniskilling Dragoon Guards (the 'Skins') is shown in a typical hilltop position during 1952 after the regiment had replaced the 8th Hussars.

on the hills opposite at ranges from 500yd out to 2,000yd. Only at the southern end of the divisional front were the two sides in close proximity on a position known as The Hook. This was the scene of repeated ferocious battles. There were three infantry brigades on the front lines at any one time with each supported by one tank squadron. Since the 25th Canadian Infantry Brigade had its own integral armour support, it follows that two squadrons of 1 RTR were at the front with the third held in reserve at Gloucester Valley where Regimental Headquarters was located.

The three brigade sectors of the divisional 13,000yd frontage were commonly known by the names of the three predominant physical features in the area. Thus the left-hand brigade occupied The Hook sector; the centre on Point 187 and the right on Point 355. Against all the conventions of armoured warfare, the tanks were positioned as static pillboxes on the highest hilltops with the widest arcs of fire to dominate as much enemy territory as possible. In general a half-troop of two tanks supported each infantry company but tanks were not

ABOVE By 1953, 1 RTR replaced the Skins and continued the peculiar role of tanks emplaced as static pillboxes on the hilltops in support of the infantry of 1st Commonwealth Division – note the divisional insignia on the rear hull of this Centurion Mark 3 at the moment of firing, with 20-pounder rounds piled on the rear decks as a ready supply of ammunition for prolonged engagements.

too popular within the company locality as they attracted a great deal of enemy artillery rounds. Nevertheless, the tanks became an integral part of the infantry defensive fire plan. By day, tank crews kept the enemy lines under constant observation and any new diggings or fortifications were engaged as targets of opportunity. In particular, enemy observation posts were priority targets as they directed the artillery bombarding friendly troops. Thanks to the accuracy of the Centurion's 20-pounder main armament, such pinpoint targets could be destroyed out to 2,000yd and beyond, depending on the skill of the gunner.

By night the tanks were at constant readiness to bring down defensive fire on preregistered targets on call from the infantry either in support of fighting patrols or against enemy probes. Such targets were registered during daylight hours but disguised among other speculative shoots to confuse the enemy. The settings on the tank's fire control system were then recorded for future reference and a round could be on its way to the target even on the darkest of nights at the request of the infantry. Some tanks were equipped with an American 18in searchlight that allowed observation of no-man's-land at night, but the device was vulnerable to enemy small arms fire and artillery fragments. Other Centurions were fitted with a .50-calibre Browning heavy machine gun to bolster firepower.

Such a routine required the tanks to be

manned on a 24-hour basis. Accordingly the crews divided the watches with often just a single observer by day and two crewmen at night, with one acting as gunner and the other as the loader/operator. The remainder of the crew went about their daily chores, including ensuring that the tank and its adjacent bunkers were fully charged with ammunition with each tank position having up to 200 rounds. At dawn and dusk, the full crew manned the tank as they did during enemy attacks. Sleep was always at a premium and any rest was taken inside the crew's 'hutchie' that was close to the tank's position. There they lived for up to six weeks at a time in all weathers and throughout the bitter Korean winter. Warmth was provided by petrol-fuelled space heaters but these were dangerous devices and more casualties were inflicted from burns than by enemy action. Besides sleep, food was a major preoccupation, but the benefit of being in a multinational UN army was that rations could be obtained from several sources beside the standard compo, most of which was manufactured during the Second World War. American C-Rations made a welcome change, but better still were their frozen turkeys and steaks. British troops had one great advantage in that they were allowed alcohol on the front lines. This proved to be a splendid bartering tool and a bottle of Scotch could be traded for a Jeep or a Browning heavy machine gun.

The tanks proved so effective in their role of direct fire support that the Chinese Communist Forces tried on several occasions to force them from their hilltop positions through intensive artillery bombardments with 76mm, 85mm and 122mm howitzers and anti-tank guns. Although many tanks were hit repeatedly, crews that were safely inside incurred no casualties. This was testament to the excellent armour protection of the Centurion. Many tanks were damaged, particularly to external stowage bins, optical devices and radio aerials, but none were destroyed. All such damage was readily repaired or the tank replaced and so their fire support was always available by day and night. On occasions this proved crucial, such as during the final Chinese offensives to capture the key Hook feature that dominated the road to the South Korean capital of Seoul. Throughout the night of 28/29 May 1953, the Chinese mounted repeated human wave attacks against The Hook that was defended by the Duke of Wellington's Regiment. The assault was broken by the concerted fire of divisional artillery which fired 30,700 rounds and the tanks of C Squadron 1 RTR which fired 504 20-pounder rounds and 27,000 rounds of small arms ammunition. On 27 July 1953 an armistice came into effect. During five months in the line, the regiment fired 23,800 main armament rounds and the tanks received 68 direct hits. It was an extraordinary role for tanks but 1 RTR utilised them to the full in support of the infantry.

The Korean War was noteworthy as it was fought by a United Nations command comprising some 15 nations that deployed military forces in support of the Republic of Korea against Communist aggression following the invasion across the 38th Parallel by North Korea. Similarly it is further noteworthy that for the first and only time a British Commonwealth division was formed comprising Australian, British, Canadian and New Zealand troops. At its peak strength in 1953, 1st Commonwealth

Division totalled 24,015 men with 2,282 from Australia, 14,198 from the UK, 6,146 from Canada and 1,389 from New Zealand. During the course of the war, 1,263 British Commonwealth troops were killed and a further 4,817 were wounded in action. This was no mere 'police action'. This was a brutal war with hundreds of thousands of civilian casualties. Yet today South Korea is one of the most prosperous countries in the world while North Korea wallows in poverty and destitution.

Suez

A Centurion Mark 5 of B Squadron 6th Royal Tank Regiment disembarks from the tank landing ship HMS *Salerno* at Port Said during the Anglo-French intervention to occupy the Suez Canal, 6 November 1956 **(below)**. The Centurions of B Squadron were involved in fierce street fighting in support of Nos 42 and 45 Royal Marine Commandos throughout the day until a ceasefire became effective at midnight. Both A and B Squadrons were landed directly from

LSTs whereas the waterproofed Centurions of C Squadron waded ashore over the beaches of Port Said during the initial assault. The black stripe around the turret was a mutual recognition device carried by all British and French tanks since the Egyptians had a number of Centurions in service. Similarly, the large white H on the turret roof was a recognition device for Allied aircraft. Suez was the largest amphibious assault landing conducted by the British since D-Day in Normandy and was the only occasion that Centurion took part in such an operation fitted with deep wading equipment.

After the UN-imposed ceasefire, the tanks

were used as checkpoints and roadblocks in Port Said as the Egyptian populace attempted to return to normality. Within days the tanks were withdrawn from the streets prior to embarkation and withdrawal. Operation Musketeer had been a military success but a political disaster for the British and French while the Suez Canal remained in Egyptian hands. Nevertheless, the Centurions performed admirably as close fire support to the commandos and paratroopers in fierce street fighting. In the words of the commanding officer of 6 RTR, Lieutenant Colonel Tom Gibbon: 'The Centurions did everything expected of them and more'. The most notable problem was the lack of a machine gun to engage snipers and *fedayeen* (guerrilla fighters) in the upper storeys of houses lining the roads, since the main armament and coaxial Browning could not elevate sufficiently to engage the tops of buildings. This was rectified in the following year when all Centurions were fitted with a second .30-calibre Browning on the commander's cupola. Here **(left)**, 01ZR15, the Centurion Mark 5 of 9 Troop with its commander and gunner sitting on the turret, Corporal Lumsden and Trooper Horsely, stands guard at a crossroads in Port Said. The Centurions of 10 Troop were named 'SHAKE', 'RATTLE' and 'ROLL'. 01ZR15 was 'RATTLE' with the name emblazoned on the glacis plate beneath the coaxial Browning machine gun. Of interest, 0ZR15 was subsequently converted to become a Centurion AVRE and fought in the Gulf War of 1991. The reader is referred to YouTube to see this Centurion and the present author in *Salvage Squad*, series 1, episode 2.

Indo-Pakistan Wars

During the 1950s the Indian Army acquired some 200 Centurions Mark 7; sufficient to equip four armoured regiments. These included 3rd Cavalry, 4th Hodson's Horse, 16th Light Cavalry and 17th Poona Horse, with 3rd Cavalry being the first. Regiments denoted as cavalry or horse indicates that they trace their lineage back to the East India Company or the British Indian Army. The Centurions of the Indian Army fought in the Indo-Pakistan Wars of 1965 and 1971. In the first conflict, the 3rd Cavalry, 4th Hodson's Horse and the 17th Poona Horse were part of the 1st Armoured Division under the command of Major General Rajinder 'Sparrow' Singh. The latter formation represented India's main strike force but at the Battle of Chawinda its offensive was checked by the Pakistani 6th Armoured Division, losing 29 tanks. Conversely, the main attack by the Pakistani 1st Armoured Division in the Khem Karan sector was thwarted at the Battle of Asal Uttar, largely by the Centurions of the 16th Light Cavalry for which it was awarded the battle honour – 'Asal Uttar'. Although the tank crews of both nations fought bravely, the high command of both armies showed a lack of expertise in combined arms operations during their respective offensives. The black elephant insignia on this Centurion Mark 7 **(opposite bottom)** denotes 1st Armoured Division as a young officer and his Sikh crew stand in front of 'NALUA', named after the great Sikh warrior and 'TERROR OF THE AFGHANS'. It was common practice to name the Centurions after heroes and battles in the Poona Horse. Note the solid yellow circle air recognition sign on the turret roof.

Both the Indian and Pakistani armies used mostly a variety of Second World War tanks during the 1965 Indo-Pakistan War. However, they also employed more modern designs in the form of the M47/M48 Patton series in the Pakistani armoured divisions and the Centurion in the Indian 1st Armoured Division. Both were highly capable designs but required extensive training to get the best out of them. In particular, the fire control system of the Pattons, with their stereoscopic rangefinders and ballistic computers, were highly complex and only useable by a minority of soldiers for physiological reasons. On the other hand the Indians used the simpler three-round battle range technique, whereby the gunner took a point of aim on the target at 800yd on the range scale and fired the 20-pounder. He then immediately did the same at 1,200yd and again at 600yd. Since errors in tank gunnery are largely due to range estimation rather than point of aim in azimuth, the three-round technique ensured a hit out to 1,400yd because of the flat trajectory of the main armament when firing armour-piercing ammunition. This Pakistani M48 Patton fell victim to the three-round technique with two obvious strikes to the turret **(top)**.

When firing from a stationary ambush position this was a highly effective method in tank engagements during both Indo-Pakistan Wars.

Six-Day War

After years of negotiation, the IDF first procured Centurion in 1959. From 1962, the Centurions were upgunned with the L7 105mm gun that was known as 'Shrir' or muscle in Hebrew, while the Centurion was called 'Shot', meaning whip. At the outbreak of the Six-Day War on 5 June 1967, the IDF possessed 338 Centurions of which the majority were armed with 105mm guns. The latter were employed in the three separate Ugdas, or divisions, committed to the campaign against the Egyptians in the Sinai. Because of their heavy armour, they were employed for the break-in battle against the fixed Egyptian defences constructed on Soviet lines, while the lighter Pattons and Shermans were used to manoeuvre through the sand dunes and attack from the flanks. These tactics proved decisive and the Egyptians broke and ran, with the Israelis reaching the Suez Canal within 72 hours. It was during the pursuit that the shortcomings of Centurion became apparent with its slow speed and high fuel consumption resulting in a limited operational range. A Shot of the 82nd Battalion of 7th Armoured Brigade shows the standard configuration of this period

least 10,000 dead. A further 5,000 soldiers and 500 officers were captured. Israeli losses were 338 dead and 1,400 wounded in the Sinai campaign. Littered across the desert were the carcasses of 600 Egyptian tanks and another 100 were captured intact. Among the latter were 28 Centurions, which almost exactly matched the 29 lost by the Israelis from a total of 122. The Israelis also destroyed or captured 400 field guns of Russian origin, 50 self-propelled guns and innumerable trucks and other assorted vehicles. The tank had reaffirmed itself as the decisive ground weapon in modern warfare, albeit with the benefit of air supremacy. Much of the IDF success in the ground war was due to the superior training of Israeli tank crews and the basic principles of employing armour in mass. Nevertheless, in the final analysis, tank warfare comes down to a young man with his eye glued to a telescopic sight and his finger on a firing switch **(below)**. That is what determines victory on the battlefield.

with .50-calibre Browning machine gun at the commander's cupola, American radio sets and crew helmets, the L7 105mm gun and a roll of barbed wire on the glacis plate **(above)**.

The Six-Day War was a crushing victory for the IDF that redrew the borders of the Middle East which still stand to this day. The Egyptian Air Force was comprehensively destroyed on the ground within the opening hours of the conflict. The Egyptian Army lost 80% of its military equipment in the Sinai Desert and at

Vietnam

In 1965, the Australian government committed troops to the Vietnam War where they operated as 1st Australian Task Force in Phuoc Tuy Province, east of Saigon. Against much opposition both politically and militarily,

C Squadron of 1st Armoured Regiment was deployed in 1968 with the first elements arriving in February, as tanks were deemed to be useless in jungle warfare. From the outset, the Centurions of C Squadron proved to be an invaluable asset, despite the difficulties of terrain and weather, particularly during the defence of Fire Support Bases Coral and Balmoral during the major NVA/VC offensive against Saigon in May. Thereafter, the tanks were used for a host of missions from route security to protecting land-clearing teams and from perimeter defence to reconnaissance-in-force. Nevertheless, the ageing Centurions presented a major maintenance task to their crews and to RAEME personnel who accompanied the tanks in the field on almost all occasions for repair or replenishment. Here we see an M113A1 Fitters Track lifting a Barnes fuel transfer pump to resupply a Centurion Mark 5/1 AUST of B Squadron with petrol from a bladder in the back of an International F1 5-ton truck in July 1969 **(top)**. Typical of Centurions in Vietnam, this one has spare roadwheels on Omega brackets on the glacis plate as ready replacements for those damaged by mines. Note the left-hand one is lower than the other so as not to impede the driver's vision.

No 4 Troop of A Squadron prepares for action with the infantry of C Company 8th Battalion Royal Australian Regiment during Operation Hammersley in the Minh Dam Secret Zone, prior to an attack against a bunker system, February 1970 **(below)**. This Centurion Mark 5/1 AUST shows most of the modifications applied to the tanks for service in Vietnam including the auxiliary 100-gallon fuel tank at the rear, reinforced trackguards along the sides and star picket welded along the stowage bins to protect the latches – as well as the removal of the smoke dischargers as they were a liability in the jungle. In addition the Mark 5/1 AUST featured an uparmoured

glacis plate, a .50-calibre ranging gun and IR night-fighting equipment. The latter was sometimes used to ambush enemy sampans plying inland waterways at night by viewing through IR sights before engaging by white light from an accompanying tank. Undoubtedly the most important role for the tanks was the support of infantry in an assault against heavily entrenched enemy positions that were so heavily fortified that they were impervious to infantry weapons and all but a direct hit from medium artillery. However, no bunker system could resist a concerted pounding by Centurions firing canister to strip away the vegetation concealing a position followed by the massive kinetic shock of APCBC rounds at close range and then HE to destroy anything that remained.

Yom Kippur, 1973

There is no doubt that the L7 105mm gun was one of the outstanding tank weapons of the 20th century. During the 1960s and '70s it was widely employed within NATO and was the standard main armament for the front-line tanks of the IDF, be it L7, M68 or the locally manufactured Shrir. It was the weapon that proved decisive in the opening days of the October War of 1973 when just 177 Centurion tanks held the Golan Heights for two days and three nights against overwhelming odds. Almost 1,400 Syrian tanks attacked with the element of surprise following a brilliant deception plan, combined with a concerted Egyptian assault across the Suez Canal. On the front line of the Golan Heights were just two battalions of 66 Shot tanks, the 53rd and 74th, of the resident 188th 'Barak' Armoured Brigade. In reserve was the 7th Armoured Brigade, recently deployed from the Sinai Desert and equipped on arrival with 111 Shot tanks from Northern Command. These formations fought the Syrians to a standstill as the reserves were mobilised in Israel and made their way hurriedly to the front. This Shot of the 77th Battalion of 7th Armoured Brigade **(left)** was photographed just hours before the war began and was just one of six that was left from the battalion at the end of the climactic Battle for the Valley of Tears.

The fighting on the desolate terrain of the Golan Heights was unremitting and ferocious. Unlike previous wars, the Syrian tank crews attacked with dogged determination, seemingly indifferent to the heavy casualties being inflicted upon their comrades. In the north, where the 7th Armoured Brigade was committed together with the 74th Battalion of the Barak Brigade, the terrain was more suited to defence and the combined Israeli forces were able to hold the Syrian attack, albeit with dreadful casualties culminating in the Battle for the Valley of Tears when the Syrians threw in the T-62s of the elite Republican Guard against just a handful of Shot Cals. The line held – just – before reinforcements arrived, at which time the Syrians retreated in good order despite their appalling losses. To the south the situation was even more dire where a single battalion, the 53rd of the 188th Barak Brigade with only 33 Shot Cals, lay in the

path of the main Syrian offensive. Fighting from prepared firing ramps, the Shot Cals exacted a fearful toll on the Syrian tanks but numbers prevailed and a breakthrough was achieved **(above)**. The roads to Lake Galilee and Israel itself were open. The process of mobilising reserves was meant to take 48 hours after due warning. On Yom Kippur there was none, but thanks to the empty roads the first tanks arrived on the Golan Plateau in just 10 hours. Thereafter tanks were fed into battle, platoon by platoon, with desperate haste until the Syrian offensive was halted by 10 October.

Much of the Golan Heights is strewn with volcanic basalt rocks and lava flows that are impassable to wheeled vehicles and difficult even for tracked AFVs. Accordingly the few roads running east to west were of vital significance to both the attackers and defenders. These roads effectively determined the axis of any offensive, so the Shot was the preferred tank for deployment on the Golan because of its heavy frontal armour and its robust Horstmann suspension for cross-country movement over broken ground. The Magach (M48 and M60 Patton) however, was better suited to the sands of the Sinai Desert on account of their higher speed and torsion bar suspension. Even so, the tracks of the Shot Cal soon became distorted and bent, which meant that it was not possible to break a track during maintenance. The problem was overcome by cutting off the

ends of every sixth track link (as seen here on the fourth track link down) to allow access to the track pins. This Shot Cal of a reserve unit is advancing across the Golan with artillery bursting in the background **(below)**. Note the spent shell case lodged behind the air filter box on the trackguard behind the turret – one of the main discernible characteristics of the Shot Cal, as is the small housing, known as the 'Villa', on the glacis plate above the spare track links that covers the external fire extinguisher pull handle.

Following the holding action of the opening days when the Barak Brigade was virtually annihilated, the IDF mounted a counter-offensive into Syria against determined opposition with heavy casualties on both sides. Of the 1,400 Syrian tanks committed to battle, 1,081 were knocked out, together with 50 Iraqi and 20 Jordanian tanks – the latter being Centurions. Of these, 867 were left on the Golan Plateau, including 627 T-54/55s and 240 T-62s. The 105mm gun accounted for 80% of the victims with 70% of all engagements at ranges below 2,000yd, while 50% of the tanks penetrated by 105mm caught fire and were burnt out. IDF statistics reveal that 680 Centurions were deployed on the Golan, of which two-thirds were Shot Cal and the remainder Shot Meteor. Of the 200 Shot Cals engaged in the first few days, each was struck on average one and a half times

by ordnance of various types, with the most damaging to men and machines being artillery and especially heavy mortars. Of those struck by 100mm and 115mm AP projectiles, 29% were penetrated, of which 25% caught fire, like this Centurion Meteor **(left)** rent asunder by internal explosion. Syrian losses on the Golan were 3,500 dead and 5,000 wounded, while Israeli casualties were 772 dead and 2,453 wounded, mainly from the armoured corps, in just 19 days of combat. The Barak Brigade suffered 112 killed in action. The Battle for the Golan Heights was arguably the greatest defensive battle in the history of armoured warfare and undoubtedly Centurion's finest hour.

Angola

During the 1960s and '70s the Soviet Union fomented many of the revolutionary wars across Africa in an extension of the Cold War. One of the longest conflicts took place in Angola and the adjoining country of South West Africa (now Namibia) starting in 1966 and continuing until 1989. At the outset it was a classic counter-insurgency campaign conducted by the police in South West Africa but as the strength of the SWAPO (South West African People's Organisation) insurgents based in Angola grew the South African Army was sucked into the fighting. Year on year the scale of combat grew

as the Soviet Union and their Cuban acolytes poured more men and *matériel* into Angola. By the mid-1980s, there were 60,000 Cuban troops and 600 T-54/55 tanks in Angola. The South African response was to deploy the Olifant MBT to the theatre of operations **(opposite bottom)**. Like the Australians in Vietnam, there was much opposition to such a move but in October 1987, the 14 Olifants of E Squadron School of Armour were committed to the Border War in Angola. Their first action took place on 9 November 1987 in an assault on the FAPLA 16th Brigade. The attack began at 0100 hours and at 0809 the Olifant commanded by Lieutenant Hein Fourie engaged a T-55, the first enemy AFV to be destroyed by a South African tank since the Second World War. Just 8 minutes later another T-55 fell victim to the Olifant of Lieutenant Abrie Strauss. Thereafter, the Olifant was to dominate every tank vs tank engagement with none being lost to enemy tank fire.

In this photograph there are three Olifant tanks in close proximity **(below)**. It graphically illustrates the problems of command and control in such heavy vegetation where engagement ranges were rarely above 150yd and more often as short as 50yd, as shown here with a target burning to the left of the picture. It also highlights the difficulty of identifying enemy troops or bunkers hidden in the undergrowth until the enemy opened

fire at close range if they so wished, although the sheer sensory overload of a squadron of Olifants crashing through the bush with their turbocharged Continental engines screaming at full throttle was often sufficient incentive for FAPLA (People's Armed Forces of Liberation of Angola) soldiers to withdraw. Like the Centurions in Vietnam, the Olifants suffered significant external damage during passage through the bush, with bazooka plates, commander's machine gun, smoke dischargers, aerial bases and so on being ripped off, while dead trees and branches (let alone poisonous snakes) often fell on to the turret roof, much to the discomfort of tank commanders. Furthermore, drivers were completely blind after the first few yards of starting off since leaves and vines soon covered vision blocks and they had to be instructed by the commanders at all times as to which way to go. In open terrain, the dust was appalling, while in heavy bush the humidity was oppressive and the temperatures often in the region of 45+°C, but worst of all were the perpetual hordes of flies and recurring diarrhoea that within the confines of a tank was less than pleasant.

It must never be overlooked that armoured warfare is a brutal endeavour with no quarter given. Every tank carries a human crew and every tank hit means death and mutilation in a most unseemly manner, such as this T-55 of

the FAPLA 16th Brigade that was destroyed by Olifant 105mm tank fire during Operation Moduler **(below)**. Initially, Olifant tank crews advanced with an APFSDS-T round chambered in the main armament in case they encountered an enemy tank, but it was soon found that at the typical short ranges of engagement such a projectile would pass completely through a target with no appreciable result, although the opposing crew would invariably have been killed. Accordingly, HEAT (High-Explosive Anti-Tank) warheads became the round of choice in any encounter, since a strike on target would result in a certain discernible hit and a subsequent conflagration. Although HEAT rounds could be prematurely detonated by vegetation it passed through, this was exploited against infantry targets by exploding a round in the vegetation above their emplacements. The other main round carried was 105mm HESH that was effective against many battlefield targets. The Olifant squadrons with their overwhelming firepower proved to be a decisive force multiplier in the final battles of the Border

War that was recognised by all levels of the command structure after years of the dismissal of armour, despite the extensive use of tanks by the enemy. On 27 June 1988, Olifant 'Five Three Bravo' of E Squadron destroyed the final AFV target of the war – a BTR 60. It was arguably the last tank round fired in anger during the Cold War.

Centurion AVREs in the First Gulf War 1990–91

On 19 June 1961, Kuwait became an independent country after 70 years as a protected state of Great Britain. Within days, Iraq claimed sovereignty over Kuwait and began massing troops near Basra while threatening annexation of 'the nineteenth province of Iraq'. The British response was rapid with the deployment of 42 Commando Royal Marines and the landing of Centurion tanks of 3rd Carabiniers (Prince of Wales's Dragoon Guards) that had been at sea for just such an eventuality aboard HMS *Striker* of the

Royal Navy Amphibious Warfare Squadron. The troops and tanks took up defensive positions along the Mutla Ridge, 25 miles north-west of Kuwait City, as part of Operation Vantage. Some 30 years later, the Challenger tanks of the Royal Scots Dragoon Guards – the successor regiment to the 3rd Carabiniers – ended the Gulf War of 1991 in very much the same place. Furthermore, Centurion tanks returned once more to Kuwait, but this time in the hands of the Armoured Engineers. Richard Swan was second-in-command of 31 Armoured Engineer Squadron in 1991 and he takes up the story of the Centurion AVREs.

'I was sponsored by the Royal Engineers at university and I relished the opportunity to spend time with the armoured engineers and loved it. So I joined the Army in 1985 and went to 32nd Armoured Engineer Regiment in January 1988. At that time, the regiment consisted of four squadrons – an HQ squadron and three operational fighting squadrons which were 26 Armoured Engineer Squadron [AES], 31 Armoured Engineer Squadron and 77 Armoured Engineer Squadron. I joined 31 Squadron as a troop commander of 6 Troop with 5, 6 and 7 Troops in 31 AES. I did about a

ABOVE Flags flutter above the AFVs of 32nd Armoured Engineer Regiment at the conclusion of the Gulf War, 28 February 1991. Most of the crewmen were younger than the vehicles they manned and the unit was nicknamed the Antiques Roadshow. Even so every AFV that crossed the start line for Operation Desert Sabre on 24 February made it to the final objective on the Kuwait/Basra road, although they did not meet any coherent enemy opposition during the ground war.

year and a half as a troop commander and then went to do JDSC [Junior Division Staff College] but asked to remain at 32. So at the end of that course I was promoted captain and went back to be 2i/c 31 Armoured Engineer Squadron. The main assets that we had within each of the troops of the squadrons were Centurion AVRE, Chieftain AVLB and CETs [combat engineer tractors], as well as headquarters vehicles. We were still operating at troop level with Ferrets, which was a great vehicle for reconnaissance, although we had Spartan APCs and Sultan command vehicles in the Gulf.

'The Centurion AVREs were a combination of 165s and 105s with no specific ratio. In 6 Troop I had two 105s and one 165 as well as three Chieftain AVLB [armoured vehicle launched bridge]. But then another troop would

have two 165s and one 105. It was all about spreading the resources so that when we were supporting battlegroups in different brigades we had enough of each type of AVRE because 165s had a dozer blade and a fascine whereas a 105 would have a mine plough, since it could not carry a fascine or Trackway. We tended to change the ORBAT [order of battle] around, depending on what bit of training we were going to be doing with what battlegroup. Accordingly, it was really up to the battlegroup commander and/or the brigade commander to decide where the sappers were to go and what kind of resources they required for river crossings, obstacle destruction or route denial. So do we need to have dozer capability, do we need Giant Viper or to have mine ploughs as well?

'We spent a large period of our time on training exercises – I mean an extraordinary amount of time – and actually far more than I ever anticipated. And that provided challenges in themselves particularly with the Centurions with significant reliability problems and the lack of spares and there were forever breakdowns of all sorts. Engine and gearbox overheating were the main problems both in Germany and in the Gulf but that was hardly unexpected given the age of the vehicles. Nevertheless, we were in the field for about five months of the year deployed with different battlegroups

and different brigades and of course we'd have our own regimental exercises as well, which we tended to do in the wintertime and occasionally a troop would support live firing at BATUS [British Army Training Unit Suffield] in Canada. So we would be doing our regimental exercises in December, January, February time up on the north German plain, at as low as -30°C occasionally. Accordingly, the vehicles needed pretty much constant maintenance, literally it was constant just to keep them on the road – but keep them on the road we did. It was an amazing experience to be still operating Centurion and Chieftain vehicles in the late '80s. We were often referred to as the 'Antiques Roadshow'. And then came the Gulf War.

'In September 1990, 26 Armoured Engineer Squadron was deployed to the Gulf in support of 7th Armoured Brigade. As I recall the squadron took only Chieftain AVREs and AVLBs, together with CETs, because there were major concerns about reliability, maintenance requirements and adequate spares for the Centurions. Even so it took the resources of a complete regiment to put 26 AES in the field. When the decision was taken to deploy 4th Armoured Brigade, 32 Armoured Engineer Regiment was included to support the newly formed 1st (BR) Armoured Division, but acting as theatre troops to be employed with whom, where and when as required. In fact, virtually all the remaining armoured engineer assets in Germany were deployed to the Gulf but attached to and under command of 32 Engineer Regiment. I recall that we did not deploy with the 105mm AVREs so the troop ORBAT was two each of Centurion 165 AVRE, Chieftain AVLB and CET while regimental HQ had newly procured flail vehicles for mine clearance.

'The advance troops arrived just before Christmas to supervise the unloading of the vehicles at Al Jubayl, while the main body of the regiment deployed and was firm on the ground by 7 January 1991. When we disembarked, all the vehicles were ready and waiting for us. However, there was an awful lot of work to do and in particular the uparmouring of the Centurions and Chieftains. The latter were uparmoured first, since at that stage bridgelaying was deemed to be the priority rather than obstacle clearance. The other major consideration was training on the 165mm demolition gun. Because of safety regulations, the Centurion 165 AVRE had not been fired by crews from under armour since the late 1960s, probably due to the end of ammunition production in Britain. Instead, the 165 was loaded by the crew in a static position at range camps and then fired remotely from outside the vehicle. We were issued with American ammunition (as used in the M 728 Combat Engineer Vehicle) and we began range practice at the Devil Dog Dragoon Range in January. I have a recollection that the first Centurion 165 AVRE to fire a round from under armour in the Gulf was commanded by Corporal 'Vinnie' Conlan. He had been a sapper man and boy and was a highly experienced armoured engineer, as were all the Centurion AVRE commanders, in order to get the best out of the ageing vehicles. All went well but it was discovered that the US 165mm round was some 2in longer than the British one, so stowing the rounds inside the AVRE was somewhat unsatisfactory.

'By February, we were becoming increasingly concerned about the late arrival of the uparmouring kits for the Centurions (both AVRE and ARV), since we were now undertaking divisional exercises training for the break-in battle. One of these was Exercise Dibdibah

Drive, which proved highly dramatic when two Centurion AVREs caught fire while refuelling and then exploded in spectacular fashion. Whatever the cause, it made us all the more anxious to uparmour our tanks. When the kits finally arrived, we fitted them in the desert with assistance from our REME personnel. At the end of the day we were fighting an army that had pretty primitive equipment and probably the most modern equipment they had was the T-72 tank. Their anti-tank missiles were not a particular worry to us, but psychologically, anything we could do to uparmour our vehicles was most welcome.

'After another major exercise, Dibdibah Charge, we moved to Concentration Area Keyes before we went to war on 24 February [1991]. I recall that elements of 31 AES (which was a divisional theatre asset) had been allocated to 4th Armoured Brigade in order to assist with the breach through the main Iraqi obstacles. In the event, after our live training in theatre using Giant Viper and AVRE breach capability, the breach was done rather more quickly and easily than anticipated and AVRE support was not required. Nevertheless, two Centurion AVREs were right in the front line in the event of an opposed crossing. Thereafter, every vehicle of 32 Armoured Engineer Regiment drove from the start-line to the Mutla Ridge. This was pretty much unopposed, save for dealing with numerous unexploded bomblets. Certainly the AVREs – once they had gone through the breach –- did not undertake any combat role at all. Indeed, the major task was handling Iraqi POWs, which did slow our progress to Objectives Cobalt and Sodium north of Kuwait City where we found the British battlegroups astride the Basra Road.

'Following the ceasefire, our CO, Lieutenant Colonel Alwin Hutchinson, pushed very hard for a high-profile task for the regiment. It was soon evident that the Mutla Pass north of Kuwait City was blocked to such a degree that the passage of logistics to the northern border with Iraq was severely compromised. As there were minefields everywhere, particularly to each side of the Basra Road connecting Kuwait City to Iraq, there was little choice but to clear the route – a classic task for armoured engineers. A preliminary reconnaissance on 1 March

Following the conflict, 31 Armoured Engineer Squadron was tasked with clearing the Kuwait to Basra road, which was an important main supply route for the Coalition Forces to the border of Iraq. Centurion AVREs were needed to clear the road of enemy military and looted civilian vehicles destroyed at the Mutla Pass by marauding A-10 Warthog ground-attack aircraft. Many of the enemy AFVs were still loaded with ammunition so it fell to the AVREs to push them to the side of the road in case the ammunition exploded in situ. Here, EASY POSSE pushes a T-54 from the roadway.

indicated that the road was jammed nose-to-tail with not only civilian vehicles and trucks but also tanks and artillery pieces all mixed up together with an awful lot of unexploded ordnance everywhere.

'It fell to 31 AES to clear the road through the Mutla Ridge [30km north-north-east of Kuwait City] using all the divisional theatre AVRE assets under the command of Major Stuart Lomas. There were some nine Centurion AVREs

and nine CETs under command. The CETs were used for hauling vehicles out of the way, whereas the AVREs were used for pushing and shifting armoured vehicles from under armour in case their ammunition cooked off, as indeed one T-72 did, but fortunately without any main armament ammunition on board. The US Army [Graves Registration Service] was supposed to have cleared the bodies from the site but the place was still littered with corpses hidden

by the carnage. We pushed over one bus to reveal some 30 dead bodies underneath where they had sought shelter in vain from the A-10 Thunderbolt strikes. Great swathes of the road and vehicles were mangled from the Thunderbolt 30mm cannon. In an attempt to escape the murderous fire, several vehicles had driven off the road into the desert only to fall victim to Iraqi minefields. It was indeed the Highway of Death. Nevertheless the actual carnage through the Mutla Pass was no more than 5km and it took about a day to clear and create a new MSR up to the Iraqi border. It was a textbook operation with both the AVREs and CETs performing very well. They were worked hard and doing exactly what they were designed to do. It was a fitting swansong for the Centurion in British Army service.

'We were extremely proud of our association with Hobart's Funnies – the 79th Armoured Division – and most of our vehicles, particularly the AVREs, carried the Bull's Head insignia. We were also extremely proud of our Centurions, some of which were over 40 years old – hence our 'Antiques Roadshow' nickname. I cannot speak too highly of the Centurion AVRE. I think it was a brilliant vehicle. We all had a soft spot for it but we also hated it because of the number of breakdowns . . . but when it worked,

I tell you, it did the job seriously well. It was outstanding for obstacle breaching, absolutely incredible. They needed a lot of hard work but were just great fun to serve on really – when they worked! Of course there were problems with it being a petrol-driven tank since it was probably the only vehicle in the division requiring such fuel, which was a major logistical problem. They were tough, durable – anything of that age must have been – highly effective vehicles for the armoured engineers of which I am proud to say I was one.'

On their return from the Gulf, the war-weary Centurion 165 AVREs were phased out of service, while the Centurion 105mm AVREs were withdrawn from service with the British Army in 1992. The final 105mm rounds were fired on Lulworth Ranges by Centurion AVRE 44BA44 on 23 January 1992 by commander Sergeant L. Elmes RE, gunner Corporal S. Heyes RE and loader Corporal R. Millet. Only the Centurion BARV soldiered on with the Royal Marines and the final BARV, 02ZR77, was deployed to the Gulf aboard HMS *Ocean* during the invasion of Iraq in 2003. Thereafter, the surplus vehicles were either given to museums or sold to collectors, while, inevitably and ignominiously, some ended up as hard targets on gunnery ranges.

LEFT Centurion BARV 02ZR77 has the distinction of being the last Centurion variant to be retired from British military service. Its extravagant desert camouflage scheme is a legacy of its deployment to the Persian Gulf aboard HMS *Ocean* during the Gulf War of 2003. *(Copyright Royal Marines Museum)*

Chapter Seven

Vale Centurion!

Almost half of all new Centurions were exported, with the largest number being purchased by the United States. Once withdrawn from frontline service in Europe many were sold to the Israel Defense Forces where the Centurion/Shot remained as a reserve Main Battle Tank until the end of the 20th century.

OPPOSITE A Shot Dalat with front rammer of the 53rd Battalion, Barak Brigade, stands alone against the backdrop of the Golan Heights on the occasion of the Shot's retirement from the regular forces of the IDF. The defence of the Golan Heights in October 1973 must rank as the greatest defensive battle in the annals of armoured warfare and it was the Centurion/Shot that was at the heart of every battle in the desperate fighting. *(Photograph IDF)*

Major General Ilan Lavie, former Chief of Staff of the IDF Northern Command, was the penultimate commander of the last Shot company to serve in the regular army of the IDF. This was Gimmel Company within the 53rd Battalion of the 188th 'Barak' Armoured Brigade during the harsh winter of 1991/92, when over a metre of snow covered the Golan Heights. He, like many Israeli tankmen, retains a deep affection for the Centurion/Shot.

As General Lavie recalls:

In August 1986, I was recruited to the armoured forces joining the Barak Brigade and went all the way from simple soldier to be the brigade commander. I was a tank commander for about four months and then went on an officers' course to become a platoon commander for a year and four months. After further training I then became a company commander for 18 months with a Shot company.

His company was equipped with the Shot Cal Dalat: the final Shot Cal model in service with the IDF. At the time the 188th Barak Brigade was the last regular brigade to have Shot, while the other four brigades had the Merkava Mark 2 or M 60 Magach.

The Shot Dalat was the first model with full passive night vision. The 105mm Shrir was very accurate and reliable in the shooting. The Shot was one of the best tanks because of its systems. From my point of view it was a very old tank. You had to be a very professional soldier with the tank otherwise you would have troubles on troubles. The turret was cramped with so much equipment inside and most of it was worn and old while the [hydraulic] oil of the turret [traverse] mechanism leaked and after an exercise I would get out covered in oil like I was in a massage! But when we did the weekly maintenance we climbed on the tanks without our boots on in order to give the Shot the respect it deserves to make them clean and shine. That is why we called it 'The Elder' since it was the oldest tank in the armoured corps. We said that the Centurion tank does not have steel armour anymore but the armour was the number of layers of paint we put on it.

Being the youngest company commander in the battalion, Alon Company got the oldest tanks and those in the worst mechanical condition. As Lavie remembers:

We got tanks that should be thrown on the garbage. They were almost destroyed because we were the youngest company so we had to start to build them from almost nothing. After about a month and a half of hard working the tanks were operational and we were posted to the Syrian frontier as the alert force on 5 minutes' readiness to move to our ramps [prepared firing positions]. After about five or six weeks we had the best company in the battalion. We then had a surprise visit from the colonel of the brigade company, Colonel Yael . . . around twelve o'clock at night near the Hermon . . . and he told us to be in readiness in 5 minutes from now: 'Take the tanks out and be ready to go to the Syrian border.' After the 5 minutes we were out from our beds and on the move. He was very happy that we were in readiness.

Following a brigade exercise Ilan Lavie was once asked what the tank meant to him.

I told him the difference between the Shot and other tanks was one main thing – the Shot tank had a soul. Like a human being if you treated it well it gave you back a good performance but if you treated it badly, like a mule it did not want to go anywhere. After I was a Shot company commander I became a Merkava Mark 3 company commander with 53rd Battalion. The Merkava Mark 3 is a wonderful tank, an extraordinary tank but it does not have soul like Shot.

But when he was assigned to his Merkava company, Lavie refused to give up his Shot so he kept it beside his office in Sindyanna Camp. Soon, though, he was visited by the Military Police, who insisted on its return. Subsequently, when Major Lavie was deputy commander of 53rd Battalion, he observed two Shot tanks being unloaded from tank transporters and immediately enquired what was happening with them – only to be told they were going to become hard targets on the Golan Heights gunnery range.

As he recalls: 'I almost had a heart attack and forbade my battalion from firing at them.' Instead he insisted that oil barrels be used as targets as it was sacrilege to fire on 'The Elder'. Even during his time as battalion commander with Merkava Mark 3, he gave explicit orders that no Shot would be used as a hard target.

When he became the battalion commander at the rank of lieutenant colonel, he ordered his staff to find him a Shot to stand once more outside his office. One was found undamaged on a gunnery range and it was brought to the battalion. After two weeks he received a telephone call from the Military Police to be told that he had stolen an air force tank that was used for rocket practice: hence it remained undamaged. Lavie responded 'Forget it! I will not give up my Shot.' He reluctantly did so on the direct order of his brigade commander, but only when the latter promised him an 'official' replacement. True to his word, a Shot arrived at the 53rd Battalion's encampment where it remains to this day. Another Shot stands guard at the memorial to the fallen of the 188th Barak Brigade with a sign written by General Lavie paying tribute to 'The Elder' and the part that Shot has played in all the wars fought by the IDF: the Water War of 1964, the Six-Day War of 1967, the October War of 1973 and the bitter campaigns in the Lebanon. The soul of Shot lives on.

ABOVE AND BELOW The author sits atop General Lavie's Shot outside the offices of the 53rd Battalion, and with the commanding officer of 188th Barak Brigade beside the sign at the brigade's headquarters in Sindyanna on the Golan Heights, eulogising the role of the Shot in the numerous Arab–Israeli wars. *(Photographs Simon Dunstan)*

Epilogue

It is that undying affection for an inanimate 50-ton bundle of steel and metal that sets Centurion apart in the pantheon of great battle tanks, as so eloquently related here by Lieutenant Colonel (QM) Ken Brown of the 17th/21st Lancers.

'I well remember the day we first met. She was quite a sight to a young budding troop sergeant, delivered brand new in gleaming green livery direct from her ordnance factory fairy godmother – and she was all mine. With her registration number 00BA69, she was immediately christened OOBA [OohBar]. I picked my crew with care. Acting as troop leader who could argue that 'Sir' must have the best, and as Sir was also 'Sarge', the combination was far too powerful for protracted argument.

'Denton, my driver, was a cheerful National Serviceman from Loughborough, and OOBA took to him like a broody hen. I was never allowed to witness what went on when her maidenly bazooka plates were removed or her engine deck was lifted. It was as if what happened beneath that coy, magnificent structure was something that only Denton was privileged to observe. He would look kindly my way and murmur, "OK Sir, you get about your business, I'll attend to 'er ladyship". Of course, I kept a close check on OOBA's health and scanned her AB 413 weekly for any sign of lurking ailment – I never found one.

'Over the next couple of years, in her multi-coloured matt painted dress like some faithful old well-trusted family retainer, she played her part magnificently through good and bad, thick and thin, and never, never once let us down. Not for OOBA the pitiful sight of lying beside the road, innards bared to the heavens, while some greasy, oil-soaked fitter tinkered about rudely with her private parts. The thought alone was too disgusting for words!

'OOBA loved to show off. She celebrated the queen's birthday one year by steaming faultlessly past her divisional commander, main armament dipping in salute, and pounded her 50 tons back to barracks again as if it were but a spring canter before breakfast. She stood docile and respectful when the then foreign secretary paid her the honour of mounting her for a chat with the troop leader, and as for administration day drive-pasts, she ate them up like the best oats and bran. Her record was immaculate, her behaviour supreme – and she had the fastest tea-brewing boiling vessel in the squadron! It was almost as if that huge steel frame knew of her own importance. There were after all the perks –- first troop tank to board a rail-flat, and to be served at the POL (Petrol, Oils and Lubricants) point. The choicest harbour area was OOBA's by divine right, and who had first call on the parking place in the hangar next to the radiator? Oh! Yes, there was much to be said for being the first in any troop.

'We parted company eventually when I moved across to HQ squadron as signals sergeant. I did not see very much of her after that, but whenever I did catch a glimpse of that somehow familiar old battlewagon, I always gained the impression that she was peering down her gun barrel at me like an aged aunt might look with faint disapproval at some wayward but nevertheless favourite nephew.

'I remember there was one particular exercise that never failed to arouse a little excitement in Germany in those days, which involved a drive across country along a rutted, dusty track called the Wieztendorf Corridor. This track was the main artery between the Hohne Ranges and the vast expanse of the Soltau Training Area, which at that time stretched all the way to Lüneburg.

'After annual firing at Hohne it was customary for the regiment to achieve this 30-odd-mile drive during the weekend, but as most officers seemed to have pressing engagements elsewhere, it often fell to the SSMs and troop sergeants to conduct the move. It was an ideal set-up. A simple non-tactical move in daylight from one harbour to another, following a well-signed track and crossing various main roads at pre-selected points, where traffic control was organised by recce troop and others. On this kind of move one could almost relax, sit back in the turret and enjoy the scenery. In a word – a perfect "swan".

'On one particular fine sunny Sunday afternoon in August, the signals officer and myself, for reasons that are no concern to the reader, found ourselves suitably armed with traffic lollipops at the point where the Wieztendorf Corridor crosses Route 3 just south of Soltau. This was long before the Hamburg autobahn was built, and consequently the route was an extremely busy thoroughfare. Feeling hot, dirty and dusty, we somehow considered it well below our dignity to find ourselves with such a menial task. However, having been promoted from the turret so to speak, we knew the drill, and at the appointed time duly raised our batons and brought to a stop the roar of the Hamburg–Hanover traffic.

'At this crossing point, the track leaves a dense wood about half a mile from the road and we not only had early warning of the tanks' approach but also a splendid view as they came bursting out of the woods like angry lions charging up the track flat out, to burst across the main road, tracks screaming, governors banging and flames spurting like thunderous bats from hell, only to disappear into the trees on the other side of the road. What a fantastic sight it was, and the watching Germans loved every minute of the spectacle.

'We had been going through this drill for an hour or so, nonchalantly waving to our friends and getting the universal sign of thanks in return from every turret – two fingers jabbing upwards –- when we noticed the first tanks of 'C' Squadron approaching. Being both ex-'C' Squadron ourselves, the signals officer and I prepared to give our old squadron the very best of crossing service and began stopping the road traffic just a little early so that the boys could really get steam up and show the locals a thing or two. This they dutifully did,

ABOVE A Centurion tank lies burnt and shattered. In contrast to 'A Cent named OOBA,' but like so many other Centurions, this tank has been destroyed utterly on a gunnery range, at the end of a noble career in the hands of devoted crew and fitters.

ABOVE A troop of Olifant Mark 2s of 1st South African Tank Regiment undertakes a night shoot during the annual springtime firepower demonstration at the de Brug gunnery ranges near Bloemfontein. The current generation of Main Battle Tanks, including Olifant Mark 2, incorporates a full solution fire control system that compensates for numerous factors affecting accuracy such as trunnion tilt, barrel wear and meteorological parameters to provide a high hit probability out to ranges of 3,000yd. This can be achieved even when the Olifant Mark 2 or the target is either moving or stationary, by day or night, as well as in foul weather due to the gunner's and commander's stabilised thermal imaging sights for tank versus tank engagements. Needless to say, when firing the current APFSDS-T 105mm rounds the Olifant Mark 2 will out-perform any gun tank in sub-Saharan Africa. Such firepower and capability undoubtedly reinforces the motto of 1st South African Tank Regiment – 'We Make the Rules'. *(Photograph SAAC)*

and for some strange reason I seemed to get something in my eye when that beautiful sight came roaring up the track, and my dear old OOBA thundered across, just that little bit faster than anyone else, I thought. There was Denton giving me the thumbs up and young Stangroom the gunner had the nerve to dip the 20-pounder as they crashed past, or perhaps that was the stabiliser playing up? True to form SHQ, 2nd, 3rd and 4th charged across the road and then there was a gap, so regretfully we allowed what seemed like one-half of the

German nation to continue motoring south while the other half sped north.

'Some little time passed and the signals officer, a young captain named Mulloy, as I recall, complained that I had smoked all his cigarettes and was about to depart for replenishment when we noticed, almost idly, an ever-increasing cloud of dense black smoke rising above the trees a few hundred yards into the wood where the tanks had just disappeared. This was soon followed by the sound of a very ominous explosion. I turned to comment to Captain Mulloy, but already he was bounding for his Champ and he took off down that track like a scalded cat. I remained to watch that smoke billow and thicken in the ever-rising clouds into the hot afternoon air, and looked anxiously for the familiar sign of the Cent ARV to come up the track towards me.

'After a short while I was called to RHQ and for a few hours the events of the afternoon were put to the back of my mind. That evening the signals officer filled me in on the details, which briefly were that a tank had stalled in a particularly bad part of the track and in thick hanging dust the following one had mounted it, splitting open the rear-mounted jettison petrol tank, which a spark from the grinding metal had ignited,

setting both tanks on fire. It was only due to the quick thinking and courage of the following tank commander, who leapt into the front tank and managed to drive it forward a small distance, thus breaking contact, that saved both tanks from completely brewing up. The fire was put out on one, but the other was by now a raging inferno and was left to burn out, despite the efforts of the fire brigade who did everything possible to save it. For his magnificent action Sergeant Etherington, the tank commander, was awarded the Commander-in-Chief's Commendation.

'I became very much involved in the regimental training during the next few weeks and it was not until one wet and windy evening about an hour before dark, that, travelling up Route 3 to Rheinsehlen Camp, I happened to pass the spot where I spent that hot Sunday and was reminded of the events of that memorable afternoon. About 10 minutes later we drove off the main road towards the camp, and were passing over the level crossing near the railway station when my eye caught sight of the pitiful hulk of a burnt-out Centurion lying in a torn-up muddy area near the loading ramp. I stopped my Champ and walked over to the sorrowful mess, that drooping gun barrel, those hideously twisted trackguards, that rusting

scarred turret face – wait! That drooping gun barrel. She had been dumped almost casually it seemed and was lying there like a drunken old has-been, covered in shame and remorse, her right track tilted up at a sharp angle as if in defiance. I shone my torch on her glacis plate searching for the number. The plate was smothered in mud and filth. Frantically I scrubbed and gradually the familiar white figures shone through – 00BA69.

'Stupidly I patted her steel skin and almost tenderly climbed the familiar route to her turret. I gazed down by torchlight into what had once been my home for many a mile, an immaculate gleaming silver-painted fighting machine which was now a morass of burnt, rusting twisted metal. The memories came flooding back and I was lost in them, sitting on that cupola in the pouring rain. My driver became impatient, "Time's getting on, Sarge," he called from the open door of the Champ. I climbed down and took one last look at her as I climbed aboard the vehicle. "Pile of bloody old rubbish there, Sarge," my driver remarked. I looked over at him. "Yes, that's right," I heard myself say, "just a pile of old rubbish. Drive on." It was just as well it was dark and raining, so he could not see the tears streaming down my face.'

Appendix

The Olifant Mark 2 represents the ultimate version of the Centurion after 70 years of development and employment as a gun tank. No other tank can lay claim to such longevity except the Soviet T-54/55 series that was always outmatched by Centurion on the battlefield from the Six-Day War of 1967 to the Border War of 1988. This table shows the characteristics of the Centurion Mark 1 of 1946 and the Olifant 2 of 2016.

Centurion Mark 1 (1946)

Crew	Four – commander, driver, gunner, loader/operator
Weight	46 tons 14cwt (92,000lb)
Length	Hull – 25ft 2in
	Gun forward – 29ft 7½in
Width	11ft 0¾in
Height	9ft 2¾in
Track width	2ft
Engine	Meteor Mark 4, 600bhp
Fuel	Petrol
Speed	23.7mph
Range	Cross-country – 50 miles
	Road – 85 miles
Gradient	35%
Fording	4ft 9in
Main armament	17-pounder 3in QF Mark 6 with muzzle brake
Secondary	Uniaxial/coaxial Besa 7.92mm machine gun
Elevation	+20 degrees to -10 degrees
Ammunition	Types – HE, AP, APC, APCBC, APDS
	Rounds – 72 x 17-pounder and 2,250 x 7.92mm
Smoke	2in bomb thrower
	2 x six-cup smoke grenade discharger No 1 Mark 1
Radios	No 19 WT set, No 38 AFV set

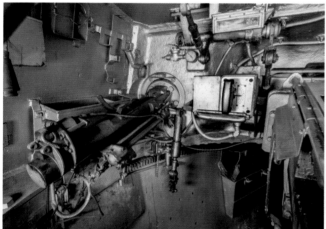

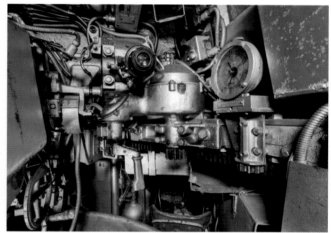

Olifant Mark 2 (2016)

Crew	Four – commander, driver, gunner, loader/operator
Weight	64 tons (128,000lb)
Length	Hull – 25ft 5in
	Gun forward – 32ft 4in
Width	11ft 9in
Height	9ft 8in
Track width	2ft
Engine	Continental Motors AVDS 1790 8A 1,040bhp
Fuel	Diesel
Speed	44mph
Range	Cross-country – 185 miles
	Road – 250 miles
Gradient	60%
Fording	5ft
Main armament	GT-8 105mm with thermal sleeve and MRS
Secondary	Coaxial Browning 7.62mm machine gun
Elevation	+20 degrees to -8 degrees
Ammunition	Types – APFSDS-T, HESH, HE/T, WP
	Rounds – 64 x 105mm and 2,000 x 7.62mm
Smoke	Engine smoke generator
	2 x six-cup 81mm smoke grenade dischargers
Radios	C21, B46 and HAR 600 intercom system

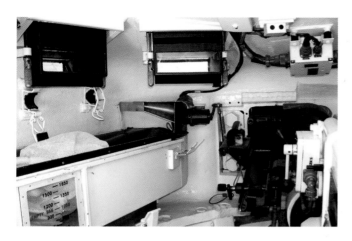

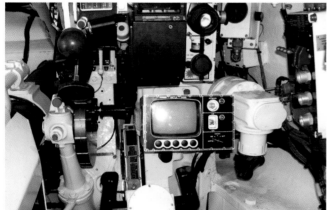

Bibliography and sources

Simon Dunstan, *Great Battle Tanks* (Ian Allan 1979)
   Centurion (Ian Allan 1980)
   Centurion War Data (Eshel Dramit 1980)
   The Centurion Tank in Battle (Osprey 1981)
   Vietnam Tracks: Armor in Battle 1945–1975 (Osprey 1982)
   Armour of the Korean War (Osprey 1982)
   British Battle Tanks (Arms & Armour Press 1983)
   Tank War Vietnam (Arms & Armour Press 1983)
   British Army Fighting Vehicles (Arms & Armour Press 1984)
   Armour of the Vietnam Wars (Osprey 1985)
   Tank War Korea (Arms & Armour Press 1985)
   Centurion Universal Tank 1943–2003 (Osprey 2003)
   The Yom Kippur War 1973 (Osprey 2003)
   Mechanized Warfare (Compendium 2005)
   The Six Day War: Sinai (Osprey 2009)
   Centurion vs T-55: Yom Kippur War 1973 (Osprey 2009)

Kyle Harmse and Simon Dunstan, *South African Armour of the Border War 1975–1989* (Osprey 2017)

The archives of The Tank Museum, Bovington.
The National Archives, Kew.

Index